Dreamtime Awakening

Healing Ideas and Wisdom to Save our Water & Life on Earth

Omileye. E. Achikeobi - Lewis

Also by Omileye Achikeobi-Lewis
(aka Ezolaagbo Achikeobi):

A Journey Through Breath

I Pray for Healing

Seven Principles of Wellness

In the Spirit of Wellness

Ploop! A Real Life Natural Pregnancy Journey and
Guide

Beautiful Waters

see also:

Humanity4Water project; along with Omileye's
wellness and healing work at www.yeyeosun.com

A Naked Truth Book
UK, United States

A Naked Truth Book

P. O. Box 461

South Carolina, SC 29720

www.aharalife.com

Design by: Adaugo Joseph & L. Derrick Lewis

Editor: L. Derrick Lewis

Assistant Editor: Remah Joseph

This book is Printed in the United States of America

August 2009

:Library of Congress Control Number: 2009908398

Thanks

To God the creator,
the ancestors on whose shoulders we stand,
the Divine Mother whose compassion makes the world a better place,
Chief Solagbade Popoola for inspiring others to contribute their greatness,
my husband, Chief Olu Derrick Lewis, who walks with me always,
my mother, Chief Remah Joseph who never fails to support me,
my mother-in-law Mimi Lewis for her unconditional love and kindness,
my brother, Jeffrey Joseph, keeps me up talking about the cosmos-stars-and beginnings of life,
my son, Kem Ra, who is the sight of the future that keeps me going,
Beckee Garris, spiritual healer of the Catawba Nation,
Chief Randall and all from the Little Horse Creek,
David Merryman, Catawba River Keeper for looking after our rivers so well,
Gary and Debbie Fourstar, of Many Horses, for sharing their connection with the spirit,

and to all those who have gone out of their way to make this planet a better place.

Table of Contents

Today I choose the reflection I will leave behind

The Circle of Wisdom

Many centuries ago men and women sat in awe under the starry night sky and observed it. Drawn in by how its grandeur spread its wings languidly from one corner of their world to another. Is it surprising that they were overcome with a feeling that there was something so much greater than themselves and filled with the over whelming question "who am I in relation to all of this?" It is a question that would echo down the hallowed hallways of generations, cultures and worlds.

Under the blinking sky the gazing eyes of those men and women would have noticed that under the stillness of the night sky was a throbbing movement of order. One that crops and heart beats danced in harmony to.

It might have been in moments like those mentioned, that the Aborigines, Egyptians, Babylonians, Native American Indians realized that we are all part of a circle of wisdom where we are one, share the same universal soul and operate on the same principles of universal existence. The Aborigines saw visions of Dreamtime. They heard its whispers wandering through the heartbeat of stories, songs, rites and sacred places. For they say it is within the Dreamtime that life and all the principles that govern it arose. Here spirits came to Earth, and chose their form as plant, animal or human making an everlasting pact, "each one will look after the other".

The Lake of Forgetfulness

If that was the pact made at the time. It seems that time has a way of fading the memory. For excitedly, in a different time, in the corridor of the inquisitive mind, the Greeks asked the same question "who am I?" It was one that led them to begin the separation of science "the knowledge of knowing" from the metaphysical. As the form of nature began to dazzle the beholders mind the science of deductive and inductive reasoning began the arduous passage of pushing its head out of the mother's womb. Now it became the mystery of the pieces of the whole over the whole that preoccupied the heart and mind of man.

It was the loud echo of the English physicist Sir Isaac Newton (1642-1727) that announced once and for all that we are separate from nature. A song that danced at the welcoming entrance of the Age of Enlightenment where German philosopher Immanuel Kant (1724-1804) took God completely out of the scientific equation. Reality could now be measured in a mechanical way, through math. Through anything other than the dance of the Soul meeting the Soul.

Millions of years of evolution was brushed aside with the sleight of the hand. The ancient pact now parceled away in a box made for everything marked as "nonsensical" and "primitive". The advancement into the Darwinian Age saw the split between science and the metaphysical world deepen. The Age was heralded in b British Naturalist Charles Darwin (1809-1882) who wrote "On the Origin of the Species by Means of natural Selection, or the Preservation of Favored Races in the Struggle for Life". The shaky platform for the advancement of Industrialism, greed, corruption, a dangerous disregard for Mother Earth and each other was set – as David Landes author of "The Wealth and Poverty of Nations" helps us to understand.

The Dreamtime Awakens

The memory of the pact may have faded but the fact that we are an integral part of "The Everything" is the enduring reality written on the faces of rocks, in ice, on the telling rings of trees, and in the Egyptian arms of light that extend affectionately down from the sun. We are part of the space, air, water and earth. We live and breathe these elements which arise from the cosmic consciousness which created all things, including us.

Twenty billion years ago is a hard time to imagine but the corridors of nature have shown that is when we may have begun. In a small dot of matter in the universe all the stuff of life was concentrated. Exploding grandly outward it hurtled dust clouds of life.

The clouds of dust clumped together and evolved into stars which in turn formed galaxies containing billions of their brothers and sisters. A beautiful mesmerizing galaxy with a tantalizing spiral body formed. On its outer skirts began the formation of a star which made all of life on Earth possible – the sun. The sun was to capture our imagination from that day forward. From the dust clouds everything was formed including us.

Over eons the planet cooled down, the surface of the Earth became covered with water and 2 billion years ago a small life form began - the Cynobacteria. It began the process of making food from sunlight with the help of the H_2O molecule (water).   Today we call this process photosynthesis. It is essential to all life even today. Organisms that cannot engage in photosynthesis eat those that can. In effect we are all eating the energy of sunlight. We are made up of a grand total of 60 trillion cells; each one contains organelles which are descendants of these ancient bacteria which entered our cells.

"Who am I in this grand scheme of things?" is the question that plagued Einstein's mind. A mind that was on the constant search to discover what the "Old One" had intended. The answer emerged from the whirling tides of his soul. Like a golden fish coming up for air came forth the formula E=MC2 – energy forms matter and matter goes back to energy (the nutshell explanation).

In the Saturday Evening Post, October 26th 1929 Einstein gives us an insight into the songs of the Dreamtime that plagued his soul, "we are in the position of a little child entering a huge library, whose walls are covered to the ceiling with books in many different languages. The child knows someone must have written those books. It does not know who or how. It does not understand the language in which they are written. The child notes a definite plan in the arrangement of the books, a mysterious order, which it does not comprehend but only dimly suspects."

It's hard to keep the song of the Dreamtime down. British Physicists David Bohm (1917-1992) agreed with Einstein's vision of the "Old One". He came to a clarifying realization that the universe is "an undivided and unbroken whole". The "whole" was the hidden primary reality (the quantum potential) that provides information to the totality of humankind and its environment.

Sacred Elements

We are the space, air, fire, water and earth. The ancients told us that each of these elements make up life. Just look at Obatala's Ladder, the West African story in the pages of this book, which shows us the unfolding ladder of DNA and the elements descending from the sky or the Dance of Leela in Indian story of the beginning of life. Is it the truth of these connections that played on Yoga Master BKS Iyengar's mind as he wrote in the "Light on Life", "just as we cannot separate the element of earth from the sheath of our physical body, so we cannot separate space from the blissful sheath. In asana (posture) we are playing with the elements. When we twist, for example, we are squeezing space out of the kidney, and on release, space returns, and space becomes renewed. Similarly, we are squeezing water, fire, air, as well as to some extent earth, out of an organ when we twist or contract. When we release, circulation comes back, restoring revitalized elements. We think of this as washing and cleansing the organs. This is true on an elemental level. What we are doing is playing with the balance of the elements, experiencing which sensation each will bring us."

On the most fundamental level we can see that we reflect our Mother Earth. For we are 70% water and so is she. When she breathes out we breathe in the very substance exhaled, oxygen. When we breathe out others in our biosphere breathe in our exhalation, Carbon dioxide. So the dance goes on over and over again. As James Hillman, a leading psychologist stated, "Even to think we are separate from nature is an illness. You cannot separate yourself from nature."

The Long Farewell

Hopefully, we will gracefully acknowledge our place in the world, draw on the ancient truths that sustain life itself, and listen carefully to the thoughtful and poignant words of Jonathan Weiner, author of "Planet Earth", "But the farewell is now before us. We are living it. Our dreams are troubled by the bomb and by the rocket. We are the generation in the doorway. We are the first generation of the long good-bye. As we look around today, we see sky, hills, peaks, and waves with a peculiar attention. We stare, as if we were already looking back. This is the planet on which our species grew up. This is the planet from which, with luck, we will step toward the stars. If we survive, and make it up there, it will be because we have acquired a new measure of wisdom, and perhaps by then we will be worthy of the long cosmic trip."

In the March 2009 issue of Merco Press, amongst various other National publications, it is stated we are living in a melting reality, "last month, scientists contributing to the UN Polar Year survey said ice caps on both poles are melting at a much faster pace than expected. A Polar Year statement said researchers found Arctic ice levels at their lowest point since satellites began measuring the northern ice mass three decades ago."

Scientists say that we are now entering a historic sixth extinction. There have been five in the past and this is the only one that has been caused by a single species – humans.

Okay, we can move to planet Mars. But can we? Besides the fact that the mighty red planet is totally inhabitable to us. Even if it was imagine what we would do to it? How would we inhabit a new planet? According to research paper "Ecosystem Services: Benefits Supplied to Human Societies by Natural Ecosystems" written by up to eleven environmental scientists and published in the Ecological Society of America 1997. If we even found a planet that could sustain life we would have to think which species to take. Then that is only the beginning – we would have to work out which species were needed to support the primary ones. That includes: "the bacteria, fungi and invertebrates that help make soil fertile and break down wastes and organic matter; the insects, bats and birds that pollinate flowers; the grasses, herbs and trees that hold soil in place, regulate water cycle and supply food for animals". Then to just maintain soil alone we would need about "50,000 insects and mites, and nearly 50,000 algae, 400,000 fungi and billions of individual bacteria."

My Story

I am the daughter of a Jamaican mother and Trinidadian father; great grand daughter of a Carib Indian male and African Caribbean female; great great grand daughter (on my paternal side) of a West African free man of the surname Achikeobi and the great great granddaughter (on my maternal side) of the famous Jamaican Maroon leader Cudjoe. I was birthed in the UK (with a stint of my childhood in Trinidad); educated in the famous halls of London University's School of Oriental and African studies where my appetite for journalism, the traditional and modern science was whet. Above all I have always had one foot in the halls of my Western background and the other in the hallowed corridors those of my forbearers.

The canvas of my spirit was shaped long before I was born but also by the delicate hands of the great women in my lives: my mother, my paternal grandmother and paternal great aunt. My mother taught me "wisdom"; my Grandmother taught me "more wisdom"; while my great aunt taught me "even more wisdom". From all I learned the power of tolerance and spiritual connection. For my mother did a short stint as a Buddhist; my Grandmother was a Christian and "seer"; while her sister, my Great Aunt was known as a Spiritual Baptist, great healer and dream interpreter. By the age of thirteen the wisdom of these women became the roots that grew me, the tree. I became a tree that inherited the gift of "sight", and the gift of healing. As that tree I branched into journalism with a leading newspaper in the UK called, The Weekly Journal (The sister paper to The Voice), worked as a Book's Editor for their woman's publication Woman2Woman. Eventually my branches spread into the field of empowering women and human potential. I eventually became an author of several wellness books, arrived here, where I am today an Eco activist, healer and health educator. My degree in Ayurvedic Medicine and Complementary Health Sciences from the Middlesex university in the UK – was instrumental in giving me a language and inroad into fusing health, science, spirituality, and ecology together.

By 2007, all the branches of my tree joined together when the power of my dreams invaded my world (they had a way of doing that). While living in the islands I began to dream of fish dying, rivers drying and the world needing help. The dreams would not stop. On many mornings I woke up feeling obligated to do something. Soon after having the dreams a respected traditional priest and theologian from West Africa, Chief Popoola, informed me the dreams represented a calling I must heed. Then I was given an ancient position as Crown of The Mother. The title I was given for this remit was "Yeye Olomitutu" – "Mother Who Heals with Cool Waters" and "Yeye Tayese" – "Mother Who Mends the World". The awarding of the position was celebrated at an event sponsored by the Trinidadian Ministry of Culture and Gender Affairs.

"What was I to do? How was I to help water and the world?" were questions that plagued my mind for some time. Until one day a clearly audible voice answered, "just go to water." It seemed like such a simple concept but it was the only answer I could hear. So of to water I went. For three months with a few people I went to the rivers. We would pray, give gratitude, sing, and talk about how we could make things better. In essence it was our simple way of giving gratitude and raising awareness. In 2008, I moved to the muddy banks of the Catawba River, South Carolina. With Native Americans, other members of the community and family I continued engaging in what seemed like the simple gesture of "going to water". It was also during this time my husband and I founded the Humanity4Water project.

From the simple gesture of "going to water" something inexplicable began to happen. My family and I began to: insperience and experience: the healing feminine grace of water and nature; the sensitized world of awareness awakens within us and the desires to be good planetary stewards intensify. In those moments I began to feel a rising sense of urgency that society needed to start caring about the issues at hand and the earth again. That we needed to once again embrace the understanding that we are all part of the same body of existence, the sacred circle; the mystic silence, and the "great memory" of the men and women who faithfully watched the night skies discovering an infinite wisdom. We also came face to face with the meaning from this verse from the Tao *Te Ching*,

Attain utmost emptiness,
Maintain utter stillness.
The myriad creatures arise side by side,
thus I observe their renewal.
Heavens creatures abound,
but each returns to its roots,

~ 12 ~

which is called "stillness."
This is termed "renewal of fate."
Renewal of fate is perpetual -
To know the perpetual is to be enlightened;
Not to know the perpetual is to be reckless -
recklessness breeds evil.
To know the perpetual is to be tolerant -
tolerance leads to impartiality,
impartiality to kingliness,
kingliness to Heaven,
Heaven to the way,
the Way to permanence.
To the end of his days,
he will not be imperiled.

Water and nature also brought my family and I face to face with the pressing reality: 1) we are in the midst of a terrible global environmental crisis. 2) Ignoring it is to our peril. 3) We have broken our ancient pact with Mother Earth. 4) Renewing this pact is the lasting global solution we need. 5) In the midst of that pact lies the importance of compassion and gratitude.

I am proud to say, within the last four years, we have acknowledged those (like us) who have dared to walk the path of the "good planetary steward". Through the Humanity4Water Awards we have honored and had awards accepted by those such as President Obama, Former Vice President Al Gore, his Holiness The Fourteenth Dalai Lama Tenzin Gyatso, Sri Mata Amma, Dr. Wangari Mathaathai of The Green Belt Movement, Archbishop Desmond Tutu, Baba Credo Mutwa, Captain Paul Watson (co-founder of Green Peace and founder of The Sea Shepherds), Dr. Jeremy Narby (Anthropologist, who works with the Rainforest Indians), Ted Danson, Prema Dasara, Dr John Francis of PlanetWalk who spent an incredible 17 years in silence after witnessing a horrendous oil spill, Dennis Nelson of Project Wet, Andy Lipkis of The Tree People, David Merryman of the Catawba River Keepers, Louie Psihoyos (founder of the Oceanic Preservation Society and maker of "The Cove"), Felix Finkbeiner, Rebecca Fowler and Lisa Moore (Publisher and Editor of South Carolina's Natural Awakenings magazine). Amongst many others.

These great planet heroes, who reflect each and every one of us, taught us: the bottom line issues that truly affect our planet, small compassionate actions really do make a difference, self sacrifice, the deep passion for life that lies within the human spirit, and raising awareness creates much needed positive action.

Signs of the Times

We know the Earth is melting faster than we had anticipated. But there are also sacred signs which reflect ancient prophecies about our global crisis. Many have ignored these prophecies thinking they were just old wives tales. But now the things being spoken about are eerily coming to pass. They are getting harder and harder to ignore. It seems that to do so would even border on fool hardiness.

My thirteen year old son, who I am proud to say is just completing a book on endangered animals, informed me recently of an ancient African prophecy that talked about the birth of rare colored animals such as the white Lion signifying the Earth being in trouble and the need for man to unify.

A few months after my son brought this to my attention I noticed a group e-mail sent to me from the Native American Affairs, South Carolina Commission, for Minority Affairs. It highlighted an August 20th 2009 story from *Indian Country Today* newspaper. The story spoke about two sacred buffaloes (one white, the other black) , who were living at an animal refuge zoo. The zoo was closing and the animals were now in danger of falling into the wrong hands. Many Native Americans had been doing pilgrimages to see the two buffaloes that they claim were birthed by Immaculate Conception. Whether you believe that or not, the white buffalo is attached to the legendary story and Lakota prophecy of the White Buffalo Calf Woman. She appeared to the Lakota two thousand years ago in a time of great strife and famine. She taught them their sacred ceremonies and rituals, gave them a sacred bundle, and sacred pipe. She told them that one day she would return for the sacred implements. Which are still in the hands of the Lakota.

She prophesied when she returned it would be a time when the Earth was undergoing great changes and humans would have to change their damaging ways and bring back the boundaries of respecting the spirit and Earth again.

After reading about the White Buffalo Calf Woman I decided to read on the African White Lion myth my son had told me about. I discovered that in 1975 two white lion cubs were birthed in the area of Timbavati, South Africa, an area where the first white lions had been spotted in 1928. Recently in 2008 an unusual occurrence happened where five white cubs were birthed in the same area. South African natives and Shamans say that this area is sacred and the white lions are sacred to this area. They also state that these White Lions bring a message to humanity that it is time to stop the inappropriate ways that are destroying the Earth and return to the proper laws of Mother Earth.

Reading these prophecies reinforced the intense feeling that has been growing with my increased awareness – we need to hurry up and "get it".

Making the Journey

My husband, who spent sleepless nights reading through the manuscript, described "Dreamtime Awakening" as an "exotic tossed salad". He said, "the waiter arrives with this salad you have never had before. He brings all these fancy condiments with it. You look at it and wonder whether it will taste any good. You put some in your bowl, put the first fork full in your mouth, and then something happens – this exquisite burst of taste fills your senses. That is how I see "Dreamtime Awakening" ".

Whether he was trying to make me feel good or not he seemed to sum up the journey of "Dreamtime Awakening" correctly. It's one of eating "an exotic tossed salad". Read it from cover to cover, or just flick it open and let the wisdom and advise on that page inspire you and the whole family to make a better journey with Mother Earth and yourselves.

~ 17 ~

In fact "Dreamtime Awakening" was called such because it was written within four days, almost in a state of dreaming. I remember the wonderful Editor of Natural Awakenings, Lisa Moore, expressing her astonishment at this fact. But that is how it was. After four days it seemed as though I woke up and it was done. Four days was really an expression of years of reading, absorbing, being, feeling, healing, awareness and opening up to the idea that Mother Earth was unfolding an extraordinarily beautiful song of awareness within each and every one of us. Mother Earth is waking us up and that is in essence of what "Dreamtime Awakening" is all about. It is the trumpet of her wake up call to walk better, be better, feel better and live in more peace, harmony, love and balance within the embrace of her, self and each other's arms.

You will notice I have interwoven my own reflections on nature, healing, and awakening with those of others. For the sake of clarity I have put the abbreviated version of my name "Omi" which means "water" under all such reflections, except in the case of the affirmations and celebration days I have put in the book, which are also part of my healing reflections. Sometimes, as humans we have a tendency to speed through our journey, run and not walk. I would urge you to meander through this one and smell each flower, observe each singing bird, and feel the warmth of the sun.

It is my hope and I am sure that of Mother Earth's that we realize as David Suzuki of "The Sacred Balance" succinctly stated "we are the world we depend on." When we realize this, "we will find where we truly belong and get on with seeking a way to live in harmony within a rich, vibrant and living community. "

After four years of doing the Humanity4Water Project and Awards. Myself and Derrick have discovered that only Compassion and love will get us on the other side of this reality we have created. As one of our awardees Baba Credo Mutwa, the Keeper of the Zulu Wisdom, stated, "we are heading towards a terrible disaster. The only way to steer clear of it is for everyone to have all hands down on deck".

It was through speaking to our Awardee Captain Paul Watson, co-founder of Green Peace and founder of The Sea Shepherds, that we became totally convinced by his words, "if everyone just chooses something to save in the planet: the rainforest, the big fish, the waters etc" then we can make all of this better."

While Dr. Jeremy Narby author of "The Cosmic Serpent" and another Humanity4Water Awardee who works so hard to help save our rainforest stated, "one step becomes two, becomes twenty, becomes two hundred". This was his way of saying that if we all do something now it will make a difference.

Louie Psihoyos founder of the Oceanic Preservation Society recently received a Humanity4Water Award. In an interview with him he revealed, "I have realized that everything on the planet has a song." He is currently making a film called "The Singing Planet".

All these planet heroes, this extraordinary walk, and nature itself, has taught us - we are all part of the Dreamtime. We can each leave behind reflections that become statements that inspire others. Just like the statements, ideas, healing tips etc in this book.

(Yeye) Omileye Ezolaagbo Achikeobi-Lewis
Journalist, author, Healer, Natural Health Educator, and eco warrior.
Omileye means "Water Gives Me Joy Honor and Dignity".

Contract with the Earth

Today I _____ promise to make a
commitment to heal my planet. I understand that every
little action makes a big difference. I also understand that
my planet is me and I am my planet. So making an effort
towards my own self-healing and understanding of how
my world and I function is a crucial part of my healing
journey.

On my journey I will keep an open heart and mind. I will
seek knowledge when I can realize that I cannot do
everything in one day.
I understand I will have days when I feel successful,
and days where I feel like I just cannot go on anymore,
but I will bear one thing in mind –
compassion and love is the key to all healing.
Both allow me to be create a deeper and more honest
relationship with myself, others and the planet.
They allow me not to scoff at the "old ways" but to realize
there is something deep, waiting for me in those words,
those stories and that wisdom.
I am open to my healing.
I am open to the Earth's healing.

~ 21 ~

Signature: _____ Date: _____

Celebrate

22nd of Every Month

Mother of the Earth Day

February 2nd

World Wetlands Day

March 22nd

World Water Day

April 22nd

Earth Day

June 5th

~ 23 ~

World Environmental Day

June 8th
World Ocean Day

June 17th
World Day for Combating Desertification and Drought

July 11th
World Population Day

August 9th
International Day for World Indigenous People

September 16th
International Day for Preserving the Ozone Layer

World Monitor Day
September 18th

September 22nd
World Car Day

All October
International Walk to School Month

October 2nd
World Walk to Work Day

October 4th
World Animal Day

October 5th
World Habitat Day

October 16th
World Food Day

October 17th
International Day for the Eradication

November 21
World Fisheries Day

December 3rd
International Day for People with Disabilities

December 5th
International Volunteer Day

December 11th
International Mountain Day

Water

Water

As I washed my face in the water of the sacred Osun River that runs southward through the ancient Yoruba lands of southwestern Nigeria, I wondered about the many thousands before me who came day after day, month after month, year after year to supplicate the river with their prayers, silence, songs and awe.

It was June 2008 and I was staying with elders whose lives were intricately tied to the mighty heartbeat of the river. When I was not staring into its waters, I journeyed with my husband and travel companions over bumpy dirt roads and became an eye witness to: dried rivers, wells running low, hunger, garbage piled high for lack of infrastructure, forlorn children full of hope, water too dirty to drink, human suffering painted onto a canvas of our own making.

After each trip, I entered the embrace of my abode, nestled close to the Osun Grove marked as a World Heritage Site. I was steeped in hundreds of years of history and a rhythm that seemed older than time itself. It was through the Grove the river flowed and where I after each day's trip washed the sorrow from my face.

My sighs echoed like the crew of Apollo 8, 1968, who saw the form of Mother Earth reveal her fragility as she rose above the lunar cycle. Commander Frank Borman later wrote, "it was the most beautiful, heart-catching sight of my life, one that sent a torrent of nostalgia, of sheer homesickness, surging through me. It was the only thing in space that had any color to it. Everything else was either black or white, but not the Earth. "The Earthrise" photo inspired a fledgling environmental movement. Its capturing of the sheer fragility of Mother Earth generated such love and respect for the planet. A year later after its release saw the first Earth Day and groundbreaking new laws.

"The perspective expanded again, to embrace all life in the universe, and all time since the creation," commented Robert Poole, author of "Earthrise: How Man First Saw the Earth".

We are part of life's fragility. We are 70% water; the Earth is 70% water too. We mirror the soul of our blue planet and the depths of its blue oceans in whose watery world ancient bacteria found a miraculous way to capture the sun and use its energy giving back another gift – one of oxygen. Our 60 trillion cells contain organelles, which contain these ancient bacteria. Our breath is the oceans breath. For it provides us with 50% of our oxygen we need to stay alive. What appears to be still waters is a torrent of vibrant moving life. The depths of our waters are not dead as proclaimed in 1841 by scientist Edward Forbes who dredged up 230 fathoms of sea in the Easter Mediterranean (a fathom is 6 feet), and came up with nothing.

Water moves in a cycle which reflects the oldest shape of mankind – the infinite zero. It loops around in a ceaseless hydrologic cycle which nourishes our cells, crops, children, blood, trees, rivers, skies and the world underground. In this hydrologic cycle the sun generously heats the liquid water in the oceans and lakes causing them to gloriously rise and condense into clouds whose shapes children love to name. Once full the clouds open like a Heavenly door allowing the rains to fall and wet the soils for new growth before sinking deep into the ground and finding their way back to the water sources on Earth.

Through this endless and ceaseless cycle 100 million billion gallons of water a year are cycled. Without this cycle it is not hard to imagine why life on Earth would not be possible.

It is no wonder that water has inspired generations. To capture its voluptuous body, nurturing, ability to civilize, provide abundance, infinite wisdom, within the image of the river Goddess Ganga, Osun, Guan Yin and others. Or to be declared in heartfelt poems as the Goddess who contains "all the secrets of the world".

~ 30 ~

Seventeenth century Brahmin Indian poet found himself at the foot of the Ganges river appealing to the heart of the Goddess Ganga. His soul ached with love and rejection. He was a devout Hindu who fell in love with a beautiful Muslim girl. Their love for each other ushered in the disdain of his elders and his banishment from their social circles. He tried to convince them of the sacredness and universality of love. But his words fell onto death ears. In frustration he went to the Goddess Ganga and staring out over her deep blue waters was moved to write,

Come to you as a child to his mother.
I come as an orphan to you, moist with love.
I come without refuge to you, giver of sacred rest.
I come a fallen man to you, uplifter of all.
I come undone by disease to you, the perfect physician.
I come, my heart dry with thirst, to you, ocean of sweet wine.

Do with me as you please.

This was one of 52 poems he wrote and collectively referred to them as "Ganga-Lahiri or Waves of Ganga".

Now instead of writing poems to the sacred element of water, being moved to give gratitude to it or to appeal to its heart beat for help - we find it more befitting to pay homage to this sacred element that has sustained us since the beginning of time with thoughtlessness and a lack of care. Instead of poetic words we create 260 million tonnes of plastic waste a year. And throw 10% of it into the oceans. With dire consequences to its rich ocean life. Its chemicals leak into the water creating a toxic soup. 44 percent of all marine birds eat the discarded plastic by mistake, while 267 marine species fall victim to its cancer producing chemicals. If we are not choking the river with plastic we are suffocating it with waste of some kind or another, building dams that break its spirit, and farming all its fish making the statistic of only 10 percent of the big fish in the ocean being a living reality.

Now our rivers and water ways dwindle to almost nothing, while 40% (and growing) of the world's population has no water or proper clean sanitation. The list of consequences for our lack of reverence for our nourishing waters goes on.

The Power of Water

Treasure is uncovered by the force of the flowing water,
and it is buried by the same currents

Paulo Coelho, Alchemist

Water Gratitude Prayer

Water "thank you" for all the good things

you do for the world and me.

"Thank you" for your unconditional love

and support.

I commit to helping spread your love, healing

and nurturing to the world.

"Thank you" water.

I appreciate you,

and because you are me,

I understand I am

also sending love and appreciation to

myself.

Omi

Affirmation

Today I send healing gratitude to the world.

Dear Water

Dear water we promise to stop building the Dams that
stop your flow,

that kill your fish,

that break your spirit.

Dear water we promise to stop uprooting

the trees that keep you cool,

that keep you pristine, that keep you healthy, and keeps
going all the life that lives in you.

Dear water we promise to stop,

putting our pollutants in you by day and secretly by night.
Dear water we promise to stop neglecting

your beauty and to start acknowledging all the beautiful
things you do for us.

Omi

The Spirit of Renewal

With water covering about 80% of our planet, one would
think that our water resources are unlimited. However,
upon closer inspection, we find our water resources at risk,
and it is not as renewable as we may think.

Eco Touch LLC, 2007

The Ocean

In the deep ocean floor the balance is gone.
The animals want to go to that cloudy home,
because of humans irresponsibility to help
nature is gone, gone for so long you got to
wonder what have we done.
That poor Clown fish has lost its common sense
to defend its home of the poisonous touch
all due to the horrible chemicals on the Ocean floor.
You got to wonder what have we done.
Sea birds look at the ocean with no enthusiasm or
adventure in their eyes.
Looking at the black oil covered ocean they can't see
the reflection of Mother Nature's beauty.
So they want to die.
Die for so long.
You got to wonder
What have we done.

Kem Ra Joseph-Achikeobi, 13

Formlessness

There is a thing, formless yet complete. Before Heaven and
Earth it existed. Without sound, without substance, it
stands alone and unchanging. It is all-pervading and
unfailing. We do not know its name, but we call it Tao. ..
Being one with nature, the sage is in accord with the Tao.

(Lao Tzu), The Tao Te Ching

Celebrate

February 2nd

World Wetlands Day

World Wetlands Day is celebrated internationally each year on 2 February. It marks the anniversary of the signing of the Convention on Wetlands of International Importance (Ramsar Convention) in Ramsar, Iran, on 2 February 1971.

World Wetlands Day was first celebrated in 1997. Since then government agencies, non-government organizations and community groups have celebrated World Wetlands Day by undertaking actions to raise public awareness of wetland values, its benefits, to promote the conservation and wise use of wetlands.

Dear Water ...

Dear Water they say you are dead,
but how can this be true?
When you move and flow so elegantly.
Dear Water they say that you are dead,
but how can this be true?
When you sing so beautifully.

Dear Water they say that you are dead,
but how can this be true?
When you can be described
as alive or dead.

Dear Water they say that you are dead,
but how can this be true?
When you sustain every single bit of
life on this planet.

Dear Water they say that you are dead,
but how can this be true?
When you are 70% of me
and me of you.

Omi

Vote With Your Mouth for the Bluefin Tuna

Yes, it's such a convenient fish to eat. We can just pop it in our sandwich, make a quick salad with it and voile! That's good for us but trust me not for the bluefin tuna. Numbers of the fish are down by 80 percent. The fish is being deliberately being driven into extinction. Why? Captain Paul Watson co – founder of Green Peace, and founder of the Sea Shepherds explained to us at the Humanity4Water team, "because it fetches more money the less of the fish there is". The politics around the bluefin tuna is reflected in the fact that on May 27 2011, the National Oceanic and Atmospheric Administration (NOAA) announced it won't list Atlantic bluefin tuna as endangered.

What can we do about all of this? We can vote with our mouths and just stop eating tuna.

Omi

Well Running Dry

Edwin Grimmel Jr. stands beside an all-but-empty, 10-foot-deep pond that spans three-quarters of an acre on his Jarrettsville farm. This is the first time it has dried up since the pond was dug more than 50 years ago.

The pond, fed by a spring, dried up three weeks ago, Grimmel said yesterday. Saturday's thunderstorms left an inch or two of water in the bottom -- nowhere near enough for one cow, let alone all his livestock.

By Linda Linley, Sun Staff ,

The Well is Running Dry

August 27, 2002

Water Magic

If there is a magic on earth then it is to be found in water.

Affirmation

I embrace reverence.

Talking With Susan Wenger

Omileye: What do you think of water as an agent of healing?

Susan Wenger: Water knows when you need it. It doesn't lose its power. You must seek its energy.

Omileye: What inspired you to reconstruct the grove?

Susan Wenger: I was just there one day to enjoy and walk in the grove. I wasn't there to change it. I was just like a child. Every time I went to the grove I had a new experience like a husband or wife has with their partner. Every time you experience that person you experience something different.

Omileye : How has the water of the grove changed?

Susan Wenger: When you have a beautiful child it is always beautiful.

June 2008 meeting with Susan Wenger, leading artist, Osun Priestess, and instigator of the re-construction of the now Nigerian World Heritage Site, The Osun Sacred Grove. Susan Wenger transitioned to the other side in February 2009

1 Percent Rules

Even though most of the Earth's surface is water, only 1% of it is fresh usable water. Ninety-seven percent of the Earth's water is saltwater, which contains too many minerals for humans to use untreated. Two percent of our water is "locked up" in ice caps and glaciers, leaving only one percent as usable fresh water.

Colorado River District, www.crwcd.com

Like Water

The best of man is like water,
which benefits all things, and does not contend with them,
which flows in places that others disdain,
where it is in harmony with the Way.

Lao Tzu, The Tao Te Ching

Water Blessing Ceremony

Do a water blessing ceremony.

Go to a local waterway,

spend a few moments in contemplation

and give thanks to water.

If you cannot get to a local waterway, then fill

a glass of water and place a picture of a chosen

waterway underneath it.

Close your eyes and

send some love to water.

Make your ceremony as simple or creative

as you want.

Celebrate

March 22nd

World Water Day

The international observance of World Water Day is an
initiative that grew out of the 1992 United Nations
Conference on Environment and Development (UNCED)
in Rio de Janeiro.

Reflections on Water

It is my belief that Our Mother called Susan Wenger decided to re-construct her Grove all those years ago, because she knew that one day us humans would lose sight of who and what we are in relation to nature and self. That nature would rebel against us and we would be in the situation we are in today.

She needed the Grove to be a living testimony and clear pointer to the power of protecting water, nature and ourselves. She wanted us to have preserved within the essence of the great Mother's body: the code and lessons to rebuilding our humanity; the way that we can live in a world that is beautiful if only we try; the importance of conviction to action; the value of working together and using the healing power of our thoughts and minds to create something beautiful.

Omi shared this reflection with Susan Wenger in their June 2008 meeting. Susan Wenger

helped to restore the sacred Osun Grove

which is now designated as a World Heritage Site.

She made her transition to the other side, February 2009

Song of the Ancients

Over and over again, the ancients prove their great
wisdom. Many traditional systems such as Hinduism help
us to understand that time is cyclic not linear. They help us
to know that there are four stages which make up one
cycle of universal time. In Hindu theology we are in the
fourth stage known as Kali Yuga. It is a time which
represents tremendous destruction. But it it is also a time
which brings in the new universal cycle which brings in
the "golden age".

(Omi)

The Sacred Hoop

The sacred hoop of my people

was one of the many hoops

that made one circle, wide as daylight and as starlight,

and in the center grew one mighty flowering tree

to shelter all the children of one mother and one father.

Black Elk, Black Elk Speaks

Prayer to the Great Spirit

Oh, Great Spirit
whose voice I hear in the winds,
and whose breath gives life to all the world,
hear me, I am small and weak,
I need your strength and wisdom.
Let me walk in beauty and make my eyes ever behold
the red and purple sunset.
Make my hands respect the things you have made and my
ears sharp to hear your voice.
Make me wise so that I may understand the things
you have taught my people.
Let me learn the lessons you have
hidden in every leaf and rock.

I seek strength, not to be greater than my brother,
but to fight my greatest enemy - myself.
Make me always ready to come to you
with clean hands and straight eyes.
So when life fades, as the fading sunset,
my Spirit may come to you without shame.

American Indian - Lakota - Chief Yellow Lark - 1887

Celebrate

March 23rd

World Meteorology Day

Each year, on 23 March, the World Meteorological
Organization, its 188 Members and the worldwide
meteorological community celebrate World Meteorological
Day around a chosen theme.

Affirmation

Today I acknowledge the Great Spirit

Celebrate

April 18th

World Heritage Day

The International Day for Monuments and Sites
(informally known as the World Heritage Day) was
created on 18th April, 1982, by ICOMOS and later
approved at the 22nd UNESCO General Conference in
1983. This special day offers an opportunity to raise public
awareness concerning the diversity of the world's heritage
and the efforts that are required to protect and conserve it,
as well as to draw attention to its vulnerability.

Water No More

Dear Water you remember that time,
when I woke up and you were no more?
I went to brush my teeth,
turned on the tap and you were gone!
I went to flush the toilet,
I turned the handle and you were gone!
I went to wash my hands,
but you were gone!
I went to make myself a cup of tea,
but you were gone!
I went to wash my dirty body,
but you were gone!
I went to cook some food,
but you were gone!
I went to wash the stain out of my clothes,
but what good did it do me?
Because you were gone!
I went to make my son his favorite cup of chocolate
but you were gone!
Water I had to do without you for a day,
but what will I do without you forever?

Omi

~ 58 ~

Water Appreciation Day

Give appreciation to water

and have a no water day.

You will learn a lot by living without water

for a day or two.

Omi

10 tips on Conserving Water

Use your water meter to check for hidden water leaks
Read the house water meter before and after a two-hour period when no water is being used. If the meter does not read exactly the same, there is a leak.

Check your toilets for leaks
If you have a leak that should be repaired immediately. Most replacement parts are inexpensive and easy to install.

Insulate your water pipes.
It's easy and inexpensive to insulate your water pipes with pre-slit foam pipe insulation. You'll get hot water faster plus avoid wasting water while it heats up.

Install water-saving shower heads and low-flow faucet aerators
Inexpensive water-saving shower heads or restrictors are easy for the homeowner to install. Also, long, hot showers can use five to ten gallons every unneeded minute. Limit your showers to the time it takes to soap up, wash down and rinse off.
You can easily install a ShowerStart showerhead, or add a

ShowerStart converter to existing showerheads, which automatically pauses a running shower once it gets warm. Also, all household faucets should be fit with aerators. This single best home water conservation method is also the cheapest!

Take shorter showers.

One way to cut down on water use is to turn off the shower after soaping up, and then turn it back on to rinse. A four-minute shower uses approximately 20 to 40 gallons of water.

Use your dishwasher and clothes washer for only full loads

Automatic dishwashers and clothes washers should be fully loaded for optimum water conservation. Most makers of dish washing detergents recommend not pre-rinsing dishes, which is a big water savings.

With clothes washers, avoid the permanent press cycle, which uses an added 20 liters (5 gallons) for the extra rinse-. For partial loads, adjust water levels to match the size of the load. Replace old clothes washers. New Energy Star rated washers use 35 - 50% less water and 50% less energy per load. If you're in the market for a new clothes washer, consider buying a water-saving front load washer

Plant drought-resistant shrubs and plants

Many beautiful shrubs and plants thrive with far less watering than other species. Replace herbaceous perennial borders with native plants. Native plants will use less water and be more resistant to local plant diseases. Consider applying the principles of xeriscaping for a low-maintenance, drought resistant yard.

Don't run the hose while washing your car

Clean the car using a pail of soapy water. Use the hose only for rinsing - this simple practice can save as much as 150 gallons when washing a car. Use a spray nozzle when rinsing for more efficient use of water. Better yet, use a waterless car washing system; there are several brands, such as Eco Touch, which are now on the market.

Don't run the tap

While brushing your teeth and shaving

Add five more ideas onto the list.

Omi

At Least Try

God doesn't require us to succeed; he
only requires that you try.

Mother Teresa,

Stick to Wild Caught Fish

Farmed fish sounds so healthy, but actually they are bad for our health, oceans and the fish being farmed reveals Ted Danson in "Oceana". He divulges that Salmon is now called "the spam of the ocean", because we eat so much of it. Most of the salmon we eat is farmed, unless stated otherwise. So what's so bad about farmed fish? Well according to Danson (and these are just some of the facts),

- Fifty thousand and more fish are crammed into the same pen resulting in rampant infection and disease.

- The use of harmful chemicals to combat those diseases. Affects the health of the ocean's waters and its life.

- The fecal matter from farmed fish settles at the bottom of the ocean floor and smothers bottom - dwelling organisms, and robs the water of oxygen, producing toxic algal blooms.

- Farmed fish often escape from cages and fight and breed with wild counterparts. Often producing freakish deformed sick off spring.

- Farmed salmon and other farmed fish are fed fish meal made from perfectly edible fish, such as anchovies, which could be used to feed millions of poor people throughout the world.

Is the Cost of Bottle Water Worth it?

Kem Ra Achikeobi - Joseph, our young Humanity4Water Polar Bear 2010 Awardee did a wonderful leaflet called, "The Cost of Bottle Water? It's a Recession Right?". He drives the point home:

- Most bottles from bottled water ends up in a rubbish dump or in the water

- A bottled water filled a quarter of the way up with oil is how much oil is needed to fill that bottle (www.nationalgeographic.com)

- Think about this, a gallon of gas cost around $3 while a gallon of bottled water cost around $10

- Plastic bottles use a lot of fossil fuels which pollute the environment

- 1.5 million barrels of oil are used to meet the demand of bottled water

- Some towns and villages have complained that within months of a bottled water company coming to town their own well has dried up

- A liter of bottled water cost around $2 while the same money will get you 1,000 gallons of tap water (

Shocking facts

- 41 billion gallons of water is consumed around the world

- Bottled water produces 1.5 million tons of plastic waste a year

- 44 percent of all marine animals eat plastic by mistake and die.

What to do?

- Buy a re-useable bottle and carry your water around with you.

Tribute to a Water Goddess

Dear Water they say you are a spirit
Elegant,
abundant,
beautiful,
wise,
compassionate,
fierce,
gentle,
giving,
nurturing,
the builder of civilizations,
the sustainer of life,
the great diplomat,
the mother,
the beader of beautiful patterns,
the maker of beautiful cloths,
the carrier of many names,
Osun, Ganga, Durga, Laksmi,
Great Spirit.

Omi

Celebrate

April 22nd

World Earth Day

The seeds of Earth Day were planted in the 1960s, when a small but vocal group of scientists and environmentalists became increasingly concerned that pesticides, sewage and industrial pollutants were poisoning the air and water and threatening the Earth.

The Ancients Said

When you close your eyes and think of the words "earth based religion" what image comes to mind? For some of us it might be people sitting down or dancing mystically connecting with the universe. For others of us it might be the image of wild eyes and faces dancing manically in some age old forgotten rhythm. And for many others there are other images that come to mind.

Whatever comes to our minds eye the truth is that for many of us the words earth based religion conjures up an image of something mystic and lost in the passage of time. However, the truth is that earth based religions are not relics of the past that we could and should romanticize about. They are high level spiritual systems that hold key scientific information on how to help the universe, Earth, and its inhabitants live well.

Omi

Osun Saves the World

One day God decided to send seventeen enlightened beings to Earth. The only woman amongst them was Osun, the Goddess of Water, beauty and wisdom. God instructed the enlightened beings to make the Earth, which was young, pleasant to live on.

The enlightened beings began to carry out God's instructions to the letter. They arrived on Earth and made a sacred grove for Oro, they created a sacred forest for Opa, and they made a small road leading to Ofe. They sent people to make Okun beads. They sent people to make brass objects. While they were doing all these things to make the world habitable and nice they left Osun out of everything.

In fact, poor Osun was relegated to just taking care of everyone, giving them food and all the nice things they needed. However, Osun knew her own power and just observed all the things they were doing. She did not protest to them out aloud but just looked on quietly.

In the meantime the sixteen men were wondering why everything they did failed. They prayed for rain but rain did not fall. There was illness, bitterness, and restlessness all over the world.

Fed up and in despair the sixteen men decided to go back to God and ask Him what to do. They left Osun alone on Earth. After a long journey they reached God. God noticed that Osun was missing. He listened to all the men's complaints quietly. Once they had finished he asked them, "how many of you went to Earth?" "Seventeen," they answered. "Where is the seventeenth?" he asked. The men looked uneasy and replied, "we left her on Earth".

God then instructed them to include Osun in all their affairs and to beg her for her assistance and all the issues on Earth will be resolved. The men went back to Earth. The Divinity of Wisdom, Orunmila, went to beg Osun for her assistance. She told him if the baby she was about to birth was a boy she would help them if it was a girl she would not.

Orunmila reported back to his colleagues what Osun told him. When Oosaala looked at Osun's womb with his awo (power of knowing secrets) he found a baby girl there. He then pointed his ado Asure to Osun's womb and commanded that the fetus to change into a male with immediate effect. When Osun delivered the baby, it was born a male child.

Oosaala was the first person to carry the baby. He petted the baby and coddled it. Then Orunmila, the father, also carried the baby. He petted the baby and coddled it and

~ 71 ~

named him Osetura. Orunmila carried the baby with him wherever he went.

The 16 men said "if someone is pounding yam without the knowledge of Osun. His or her pounded yam will not be smooth. If someone is preparing Oka food without involving Osun in it, his/her food will not come out fine. We will involve Osun in whatever we do. We will involve Osun in all our deliberations. Our Great Mother, who must be present at every important deliberation. Divined for Osun Segesi owner of a hair comb decorated with Iyun. When she was in a secret place, she spoiled the sacrifice of other divinities. Who is performing sacrifice without involving the owner of sacrifice? Osun, whose other name is Ewuji, we are all on our knees begging you. Let us all kneel and prostrate before women. We are all born by women. Before we become recognized as human beings.

Adapted by Omi from the sacred Yoruba Ifa story from Ose Etura.

The End of Living

The Whites, too, shall pass - perhaps sooner than other
tribes. Continue to contaminate your bed, and you will one
night suffocate in your own waste. When the buffalo are
all slaughtered, the wild horses all tamed, and the secret
corners of the forest heavy with the scent of many men,
and the view of the ripe hills blotted by talking wires:
Where is the thicket? Gone. Where is the eagle? Gone. And
what is it to say goodbye to the swift and the hunt? It is
the end of living and the beginning of survival."

*Chief Joseph, Wal-lam-wat-kain (Wallowa) band of Nez Perce,
18th Century*

Affirmation

Everything is beautiful.

Give Fish a Break

Since the 1950s, we have reduced the population of many types of fish by almost 90%. Sylvia Earle renowned oceanographer and National Geographic explorer – in-residence says, "Give fish a break". Put simply - stop eating fish for a while.

Melting Glaciers

Glaciers are melting, sea levels are rising, cloud forests are drying, and wildlife is scrambling to keep pace. It's becoming clear that humans have caused most of the past century's warming by releasing heat-trapping gases as we power our modern lives. Called greenhouse gases, their levels are higher now than in the last 650,000 years.

National Geographic

It's Our World

The World is yours.

Archbishop Desmond Tutu, from August 2008 Fetzer
Institute event Western Michigan University

Celebrate

May 3rd

International Dawn Chorus Day

International Dawn Chorus Day is the worldwide
celebration of Nature's daily Miracle.

The Dying of Sacred Waters

As the world observes Water Day, 2007, experts from World Wildlife Fund for Nature (WWF) warn that the world's mightiest rivers are dying, threatening the livelihoods of millions of people. It's a crisis sweeping all major rivers in the world.

The five most threatened rivers of the world are the River Ganga, China's River Yangtze tops the list, followed by River Salween in Burma, and River Indus that flows through India and Pakistan. The Ganga is at a fragile number four, followed by River Mekong, which that feeds most of South-East Asia.

The WWF report makes it clear that water extraction, dams, and climate change are the top three threats faced by the world's rivers.

The shrinking of the Ganga will lead to a loss of water-based livelihoods. The Sunderbans or the Ganga delta located mainly in Bangladesh and parts of Bengal is the most affected because 60 per cent of the water there is now diverted through dams for farming.

Omi

Honor Song to Catawba People and River

They

danced,

fished,

loved,

courted,

married,

prayed,

lived,

cried,

and

were called after

your mighty banks

O Great Catawba.

Omi

The Catawba Native American are named after the

mighty Catawba River of South Carolina.

It is now the most

endangered rivers in

*The United States according to the **American Rivers Organization***

Celebration of Mother Ganga

Dear Water
They said they would no longer celebrate you
That you are dying.
They said their mother is dying,
and what is everyone going to do?
They said how could they celebrate their dying mother?
The mother who has loved, cared for them all these
Millenniums.
They said, how could they put flowers on you,
when you are dying.
What would those flowers represent?
A dance of life,
or the dance of death?
They said they will not
accept their mother is dying,
They would rather take their own life
before they let anyone celebrate your death.

*Omi - in honor of the ancient River Goddess Ganga of India and
the Saddhus (holy men) who protested at the pollution of her
Ganga River through a threatened boycott of the renowned
Ganga 2007 festival.*

A Mighty Lake

40 years ago, Lake Chad was 25,000 sq. km and the daily fish catch was some 230,000 tons; it was fondly referred to by locals as the "ocean". Now it is 500 sq. km with a catch of barely 50,000 tons. Now reduced rainfall and damming of the rivers of Log One and Chari which empties into the lake means only half of the water now gets into the lake.

What used to be an abundant lake creating joy and sustenance for all, now has fishermen arguing about borders. With the 30 mile strong shoreline communities are now competing for access to water and pastures.

BBC News Website January 2007 on Lake Chad

Together We Can Heal Our Planet

If you wish to go quickly, go alone.

If you wish to go far, go together.

African proverb

Reflections on a Sacred Water Grove

I stood

in my Mother's Sacred Grove.

I was reminded how much the

Ancient River Goddess, Osun

reminds us that great beauty

is created with the pulling together

of the human spirit and the state of humanity'

souls reflected in the mirror of water.

Omi

In honor of Susan Wenger who transitioned in February 2009

A Tear for Every Fish

Dear Water,
they loved to play in you.
You know your children?
You know the ones that are dying,
the ones that can no longer breath your
beautiful aura, or have a home that is safe.
Now I dream of them on land looking out at
you wistfully. Wanting to jump right on in
but afraid of the only home they know,
the only home that they can call home,
they line the bottom of the rivers,
they line the graveyards of the ocean,
they die silently hoping that
one day their mother will be a safe
home once again.

In honor of the fish, river dolphins, whales,
And salmon that are dying from pollution,
cancer and over damming.

Omi

Oh Fish

A veterinary pathologist at the University of Montreal says one in four Beluga whales in the St. Lawrence River are dying of cancer. The new study says the cancer is linked to toxic emissions from aluminum smelters which dot Quebec's Saguenay region. Martineau says the Belugas are being poisoned by polycyclic aromatic hydrocarbons (PAH). Martineau reveals PAH are a carcinogen. They are produced and released by aluminum smelters. Martineau says whales feed on sediment at the bottom of Feeder Rivers, which have been polluted by companies, including Alcan.

CBC 2002, Belugas dying of Cancer

A Drop of Reverence

"It's one thing to approach water stewardship in a cerebral way, armed with environmental data and dos and don'ts, It's another to act from the deep reverence those experiences in or beside water gives rise to. The most powerful changes come from reverence. You protect what you revere."

Eoin Finn, yoga teacher

The Salt of Water

Eight of the 10 largest cities on Earth have been built beside the sea. They rely on underground reservoirs of fresh water floating, within the porous rocks, on salt water which has soaked into the land from the sea.

As the fresh water is sucked out, the salt water rises and can start to contaminate the aquifer. This is already happening all over the world.

As the sea level rises as a result of climate change, salt pollution in coastal regions is likely to accelerate.

George Monibiot, Heat

My Darling

They say a river system dies from its mouth.

And if you ever need proof of the desperate state of our once great Murray Darling, it's where it flows into the ocean at a place called the Coorong.

The Coorong is a hauntingly-beautiful wetland, an area renowned for its plentiful birdlife and rich farmlands, a place so enchanting it inspired the classic movie Storm Boy.

But now the Coorong is dying - the wildlife's vanishing - entire communities disappearing - and we're to blame.

You see, for almost 200 years we've plundered the Coorong's lifeblood, the Murray-Darling.

And, with the recent drought, we've all but sucked it dry.

This week the Rudd Government announced a multi-billion-dollar rescue bid for the Murray-Darling but, as Charles Wooley reports, for the Coorong, it may be too little, too late.

River's End (Murray Darling, Australia) Charles Wooley, Sunday 4 2008

Fishing for Rubbish

Their occupants no longer try to fish. It is more profitable to forage for rubbish they can salvage and trade - plastic bottles, broken chair legs, rubber gloves - risking disease for one or two pounds a week if they are lucky.

On what was United Nations World Environment Day, the Citarum, near the Indonesian capital of Jakarta, displayed the shocking abuse that mankind has subjected it to.

Is This The World's Most Polluted River, (The Yangtze River)
Richard Shears, 25th June 2008

Affirmation

Today I send love to water.

Celebrate

May 22nd

International Day for Biodiversity

Water Me

Two hundred million people [are] facing a waterless future. The groundwater boom is turning to bust and, for some, the green revolution is over.

Fred Pearce author of When the Rivers Run Dry, Fred Pearce and New Scientist's environment consultant, travels around the world trying to assess the state of our water resources.

Red Waters

There's a joke in China today that you can tell what colors are in fashion by looking at the rivers.

CHINA: Ravaged Rivers by, Jane Spencer, Wall Street Journal
August 22nd, 2007

In the Beginning

In the beginning of all things, wisdom and knowledge
were with the animals, for Tirawa, the One Above, did not
speak directly to man. He sent certain animals to tell men
that he showed himself through the beast and that from
them, and from the stars and the sun and moon should
man learn. All things tell of Tirawa.

Eagle Chief (Letakos-Lesa) Pawnee

The Connection

If people are not aware.

If they don't feel a connection,

they can't do anything to help.

No great change can be made.

*Erin Fowler, a senior photography major and creator of the
Catawba River series featured at locations such as the Charlotte
Museum*

Say My Name

In April 2008 the environmental group American Rivers named the Catawba-Wateree River situated in North and South Carolina "the most endangered river in America.". Among the reasons cited for the river's condition are the drought, the presence of 11 hydroelectric dams, global warming, and unchecked development along its banks. On June 11, 2008, South Carolina Gov. Mark Sanford signed legislation denoting the Catawba as a State scenic river. The designation carries no land-use restrictions.

Omi

In January 2009 the first ever Water Blessing Ceremony was done of the Catawba River by Humanity4Water in partnership with the Catawba Nation. The purpose- to raise awareness and improve the connection between humanity, water and the environment.

Plant a Fish

To commemorate what would have been his grandfather's
100th birthday, Fabian Cousteau's founded Plant a Fish.
His grandfather Jacques Cousteau's, famous ocean
explorer, would have been proud of him. The aim is to
"replant" key aquatic species back into water. If you want
to be part of this great initiative then visit
www.plantafish.org.

Moon Thoughts

We may take the Moon for granted,
but we are all mesmerized by its ethereal beauty.
The ancients related it to the element of water.
The Goddess figure in most ancient cultures has a
relationship to the Moon.
The moon was a great source of many stories.
It was also used as a marker for calendars.
For instance, the Babylonian month commenced at new
moon and the Hebrew calendar was structured around
lunar cycles. Today's Christian festival of Easter is lunar,
falling on the first Sunday after the full moon.
The Gravitational pull of the moon accounts for 70 percent
of tidal swelling, with the sun being responsible for the rest.
We are 70% water and also respond to the subtle but
powerful energy of the Moon.
It has been found that animals are affected by the moon.
Scientists discovered that the production of the hormone
Thyroxin is triggered by a specific new moon in the
northern-hemisphere.
Bees are also more active during the full moon and
the water within plants respond to the phases of the moon
as every farmer knows.

Omi

The Dark Moon – New Moon Phase

A dark moon is invisible to us. It occurs when the Earth, moon and sun are in a straight line, with the moon in the middle. It relates to the end of and the beginning of a new one. For the moon separates from the sun, and forms a beautiful elegant shining curve in the evening sky. This is a good time to examine things in your life that are at an important point of change. The Maori believe that the moon dies at the end of its cycle and returns back to the lake of Gods which has the power to bring things back to life. When the Moon returns to this lake it is renewed and restarts its cycle. This belief and story mirrors the passage of the dark moon which awakens into the waxing moon.

Omi

Dark Moon Exercise

1. Slow down.

2. Review what it is in your life you would like to let go.

3. Begin the process of releasing those things.

4. Throw out old things from the past that are no longer serving you.

5. Choose to do things that are renewing for yourself and the planet.

Omi

Affirmation

I let go of the past.

Waxing Moon Phase

Waxing moon is a time of growth and expansion. The slender crescent of the moon begins to fill out getting closer to a sphere shape. At the waxing moon you begin to feel that you want to start new creative projects. You get new ideas. You may also want to start a new relationship, exercise regime or hobby. It is a time when you can encourage your finances to grow. The waxing moon goes transits into the full moon.

Omi

Waxing Moon Exercise

Continue to make positive transformations in your life.

Observe the new growth in nature.

Find a quiet place to meditate and imagine the milky white nourishing energy of the moon flowing through your body.

Do something positive for someone else or something in nature.

Omi

Affirmation

I am flowing with life.

Full Moon Phase

Full moon is when the moon is at its most powerful. This is a time of inspiration, celebration of life especially the things you have achieved. It's a time when everything in nature in celebrating.

Do not prune bushes or cut back plants at this time as they will not grow back much in the waning phase to come.

Omi

Full Moon Phase Exercise

1. Celebrate with a candlelit bath.

2. Do a gratitude prayer to your guiding spirits.

3. Do a gratitude prayer to Great Spirit by whichever name you call it.

4. Enjoy the beauty of the moon.

Omi

Cherokees and Moon Celebrations

The modern calendar year is made up of 12 months although there are 13 moon cycles to each year. In the ancient times the Cherokee also known as the Ah-ni-yv-wi-ya centered their ceremonies on the 13 moon cycles. These ceremonies were seen as important to spiritual growth, community togetherness and being in balance with nature. The number 13 was significant to the Cherokees as it corresponded to the moon cycles and to the 13 scales found on the back of turtle's shell. As a result, the back of the turtle shell became associated with the 13 moon cycles.

The Modern Cherokee moon cycle calendar has twelve moon cycles and looks like this:

Cold Moon: January - time for purification and fasting.

Bone Moon: February - time for traditional family feast of departed ones.

Windy Moon: March -Traditional start of the new cycle of planting seasons or Moons. It is also the time of the "First New Moon" of the new seasons.

Flower Moon: April – time when the first plants of the season come out. New births are customary within this time frame. The first new medicine and herb plants come out too.

Planting Moon: May - time when families traditionally prepare the fields and sow them with the stored seeds from last season. Time for Corn Dance.

Green Corn Moon: June - time when first signs of the "corn in tassel", and the emerging of the various plants of the fields. People traditionally begin preparations for the upcoming festivals of the ensuing growing season.

Ripe Corn Moon: July – time when the new produce of what had been planted and the roasting ears of corn are ready. The cycle's festivals begin. Thanks is given to the Earth Mother and the spirit that gives to all.

Fruit Moon: August – time when foods of the trees and bushes are gathered. The various "Paint Clans" begin to gather many of the herbs and medicines for which they were historically know. Green Corn festival commences.

Nut Moon: September – time of the Ripe Corn Festival held in the early part of this moon. It acknowledges Selu the spirit of the corn. Selu is thought of as First Woman. The festival respects Mother Earth as well for providing all foods during the growing season. This is also a time when the "Brush Feast Festival "occurred, fruit and nuts were gathered and hunting commenced.

Harvest Moon: October - Time of traditional "Harvest Festival".

Trading Moon: November – time of trading and bartering for goods and produce from hunting. The Friendship Festival, when new friends are made, occurs.

Snow Moon: December – time when Vsigiyi, the Snow Man Spirit brings cold and snow for Earth. Families began to store things for next cycle of seasons and many ancient stories were re-told.

Omi

Adapted from Wikipedia and 13 Moons on The Turtle's Back, A Native American Year of Moons, Joseph Bruchac

Affirmation

I am at peace.

Rain Dance

The Rain dance is a ceremonial dance that is performed in order to invoke rain and to ensure the protection of the harvest.

Various interpretations of "rain dances" can be found in many cultures, from Ancient Egypt to certain Native American tribes. They could still be found in the 20th century Balkans, in a ritual known as Paparuda (Romanian) or Perperuna (Slavic).

Omi

Family Rain Dance Game

1. Adults drum and play music, display art and pictures of rain, and the environment.
2. Get the children into a circle.
3. Discuss Native American games. "
4. Try doing the game "Rain." Discussed in www.teachersidea.co.uk. Apparently it was played by the Northwest coastal Native Americans. They made up a game, creating the sound of a rain storm using the wooden floor. You can:
5. Ask the children what comes before rain. Explain the wind picks up and have the children make circular motions on the floor.
6. Then explain small drops of rain come next. Make the sound with the finger tips tapping the floor.
7. Now make the sound of the rain coming harder with the fingertips again.
8. Explain the harder rain comes last. Make this sound by banging the palms of your hand on the floor.
9. Reverse the order of the game.
10. You can get real dramatic with the game by clicking your fingers, clap hands on thighs and stamp feet.

--Omi

The Festival of Color

In India, as in many ancient cultures, the calendars were based on sun and lunar cycles. The lunar month ran from new moon to new moon, culminating with the Full Moon known also as Purima. The festival Holi Purinma was founded to celebrate the Full Moon season and the coming of Spring. Taking place in the month of February-March it is a very exciting colorful ceremony full of mythology and symbolism.

The story that is re-enacted and surrounds the festival goes something like this:

One day an evil demon, ruler of Heaven, Earth, and hell forced everyone to worship him as a god. He had a little son called Prahlad. This son did not follow his father's wicked ways. Instead he stayed true to Lord Vishnu, the Supreme God. However, this made his evil father very angry. So angry that he wanted his son dead. In his evil rage he sent his wicked sister known as Holika (whom the festival is named after) to kill the young boy. Holika had one trait – she could not be killed by fire. She pursued the young Prahlad and took him into a raging fire. But Vishnu intervened. He saved Prahlad and as a punishment Holika burned in the flames.

Omi

~ 115 ~

Try it

Why not incorporate elements of the Holi Festival into your own spring time celebrations.

Omi

Celebrate

May 23rd

World Turtle Day

World Turtle Day was initiated in 2000 by the American Tortoise Rescue, a turtle and tortoise rescue organization founded in 1990 in Malibu, California. The group brings attention to turtle conservation issues and highlights ways each of us can help protect these gentle but jeopardized animals.

The Breath of the Oceans

Pesticides sprayed on crops hundreds of kilometers inland can often end up in nearby streams and eventually into our oceans. Garbage can also make its way into the sea. It is crucial that we protect the health of our oceans, so that we can also protect our planet.

Omi

The Breath of the Oceans II

Oceans help regulate climate.

Their currents absorb heat in the summer and release it in the winter. Water heats up more slowly than land, but holds its heat longer.

Oceans supply huge amounts of oxygen.

Ocean plants (especially tiny phytoplankton) provide more oxygen than rain forests - between 30 - 50% of the planet's supply.

Oceans supply most of our water.

Water moves around in an everlasting circle called the hydrologic cycle. It begins when the sun's heat changes water to vapor (evaporation). Plants also give off vapor through their leaves. Then, when the vapor cools, it falls to Earth as rain, snow, or sleet. The oceans play a huge part in this cycle: each year, about 330,000 cubic km of water evaporate from oceans! (The salt stays behind, by the way). In all, oceans provide 97.5 per cent of the Earth's water and cover about 75 per cent of its surface.

Omi

Waning Moon Phase

When the moon begins to wane we enter a period of withdrawal, decrease and turning inward. The graceful

Sphere of the moon begins to gradually fade away until only the wane crescent appears in the dawn.

This is a good time for undoing, ridding and expelling negative things from our lives, emotions, bodies and planet.

It was also said to be a highly spiritual time that was associated with the ability to tune into the spiritual side of nature and life.

Omi

Waning Moon Exercise

This is a wonderful time to free yourself of negative emotions.

Do the following:

Find a quiet space.

Play some music of your choice.

Inhale and exhale until you are completely relaxed.

As you sink deeper into relaxation feel all your tension, and negative emotions floating away with your out-breath.

Omi

Affirmation

I am at one with the grace of God.

Help a Dolphin

Dolphins are magnificent, loving and sentient creatures. They are also going extinct quickly. Help save the dolphins and other big fish by supporting The Sea Shepherds at www.seasheperd.org and the Oceanic Preservation Society at www.opssociety.org.

Majestic

Israel's Dead Sea is, ironically, as old as life itself. Hidden in the world's deepest valley and protected by majestic desert mountains, the Dead Sea is one important feature in a land of mysteries, miracles and biblical legends that we must see before it's too late. In another three decades, the evaporating Dead Sea could possibly become the dry sea.

The Dead Sea is Evaporating and Shrinking.

ABC News, Nov 24th 2005

Water Meditation for Awareness

Spend time by a waterway.

Silent your thoughts with gentle

slow breathing.

Close your eyes,

be quiet,

just tune into

the sounds of the water,

the swaying of the trees surrounding it,

the inhalation and exhalation of nature.

On each in-breath take in

the restorative essence of water.

On each out-breath,

release all your tension.

Omi

Healing Water Meditation

Water is related to the Sacral Chakra,
one of seven major energy points in the body.
It helps us to remain fluid,
creative, flexible and emotionally balanced in life.
When we experience a shock or
repression of emotions,
the Sacral Chakra becomes imbalanced
leading us to feeling less creative, joyful and flexible in life.
We are less flexible, creative, and joyful.
To live a balanced life, it is important to restore this energy
center.
Find a quiet space,
play some gentle music.
Inhale and exhale gently.
On your inhalation breathe in the color orange. It is the
color of the Sacral Chakra.
Allow the warmth of the color to fill you up.
On your exhalation release all your tension, emotions and
Affirm "I embrace my uniqueness".

Omi

Happiness Water Crystals

When we showed water the word "happiness" it formed
crystals with well-balanced shapes like beautifully cut
diamonds. On the other hand, water exposed to the word
"unhappiness" resulted in broken and unbalanced
crystals. That water seemed to have tried hard to form
crystals, but it exhausted its strength and crashed,
happiness slipping away from it.

Masaru Emoto, The True Power of Water

Healing Water Meditation for our Children

Close your eyes.

Breathe in gently allowing your breath to fill up your stomach like a balloon. Pause. Gently pull your stomach in allowing your breath to be released. On every out-breath feel each part of your body becoming relaxed.

Once you feel completely relaxed imagine you are in a forest. It is very sunny, full of beautiful trees, colorful flowers, and the sweet sound of birds singing. Begin to explore the forest for a while. As you do so you see a beautiful wise looking woman. She takes you to a very blue sparkling lake. You touch the water and it feels like silk. You drink the water and it taste delicious. You decide to bathe in the water. A beautiful mermaid appears. She gives you a mysterious looking box and tells you it has something special inside that will help you with your life. You take a peek inside. What do you see? When you are ready, you come out of the water and slowly open your eyes.

Omi

Songkran Water Festival

Thailand's most celebrated festival is the Songkran
Festival. It starts April 13 and lasts for 3 - 10 days,
depending on where you are in Thailand. The word
Songkran is from Sanskrit meaning the "beginning of a
new Solar Year", although nowadays Thailand celebrates
the New Year on 31 December.

The Thai people celebrate this festival with water.
Everyone gets soaking wet and since it is the hottest
season of the year, the custom is seen as refreshing. It is
seen as a public spring cleaning day. This is a time for old
things to be thrown away. Keeping them is seen as inviting
bad luck.

During the afternoon of the 13th, Buddha images are
bathed as part of the ceremony. Young people also pour
scented water into the hands of elders and parents as a
mark of respect while seeking their blessings. In ancient
days, old people were actually given a bath and clothed in
new clothes presented by the young folks as a token of
respect for the New Year.

Omi

Affirmation

I embrace the feminine within.

Loy Krathong Water Festival

Loy Krathong is a festival celebrated annually throughout Thailand. It is held on the full moon of the 12th month in the traditional Thai lunar calendar. In the western calendar this usually falls in November.

"Loy" means "to float". "Krathong" is a raft about a hand span in diameter traditionally made from a section of banana tree trunk (although modern-day versions use specially made bread 'flowers' and may use Styrofoam), decorated with elaborately-folded banana leaves, flowers, candles, incense sticks, etc.

In the evening, many people will go to their local klong (canal) or river to float their krathongs. They believe this will bring them good luck. By the end of the evening, there are hundreds of flickering lights bobbing up and down on the water. Quite often there are also firework displays as well as shows and beauty contests for everyone. Overall it is really a memorable evening.

Omi

Tibetan Bathing Festival

The Tibetan Bathing Festival takes place the 27th day of the 7th lunar month.

On this starlit night Tibetan people take a ceremonial wash in the waters of their local rivers or natural springs. This is a beautiful and tranquil festival.

It is believed when the sacred planet Venus appears in the sky, the water in the river becomes purest and cures diseases. Venus appears in the sky for one week and all the people in Tibet go into the river for bathing.

Omi

When I Dreamed

I dreamed of an ancient land
of eagles,
I woke up and knew it was you.
I dreamed about the healing,
I knew that it was you.
When I had a chance to taste your cool,
pristine pleasures,
I had no doubt in my mind - it was you.
When we played the healing flute to soothe
your spirit,
I knew that it was you.
When we played the drum to help
your dance of love,
I knew that it was you.
When I saw the smiles on the children's' faces,
I knew that it was you.
When I went away and felt healed,
I knew that it was you.

*Omi - In honor of the Healing Springs, Blackville South
Carolina, a sacred Native American healing site that
has been healing many for centuries. In April 2009's Water
Blessing Humanity4Water teamed up with Little Horse Creek to
bless the springs.*

Do a Water Festival

Do your own Water Festival.

Omi

The Divine Mother

The Divine Mother is represented in all cultures where she is personified as water. Through the mirror of water she teaches us how to live with compassion, abundance, grace, creativity, laughter, wisdom and balance.

The ancients say the world would be a better place If we just follow her perfumed watery trail.

Omi

Make Medicinal Water

Water has been renown in many ancient cultures for its medicinal properties.

Today there are many companies selling water that has been "made medicinal" for quite a bit of money.

You can create your own medicinal water and it won't cost you a thing.

Directions

Fill a bottle of water with spring water

Label "I love you on to it along with your healing request"

Leave the label on for a few days.

Speak positive words of gratitude to the water.

That's it. You have medicinal water!

You can also add various gem stones or fresh flowers to your water. If you add gems your water will be a gem essence. The adding of flowers will create a flower essence. (look in a good book shop for books on gems and the medicinal use of flowers).

Omi

~ 136 ~

Gratitude to My Mother

Dear Mother,

Thank you for nurturing me,

cooling me,

loving me,

filling me with the perfume of

your creativity,

the aura of your abundance,

your medicinal waters,

your strength,

your wisdom.

Thank you for guarding the world

for my children,

your children,

our children.

Thank you for ensuring,

the hope that sits on

your peacock crown,

Omi

~ 137 ~

The Water Thanks Giving Festival

Takes place in Tibet and takes place on March 6 of the lunar calendar. The festival is mainly celebrated to pray for rain and children. A Lama (Buddhist teacher) brings frogs, snakes, and toads made of sticky rice with him. Each family sends one or two representatives. The Lama prays for rain while placing the frog in water, while married women without children pray for children.

Omi

The Splashing Water Festival

For three days in mid April, each year China has the Splashing Water festival. Filled with festivities and activities such as the dragon boat race, people enjoy this event to its fullest with dancing and singing.

The first day of the festival includes dragon boat races. painted with bright, beautiful colors individuals cheer for their favorite team. The second day is the grandest. Everyone carries buckets and basins in the street and spray each other. The person who gets the wettest is said to be the luckiest participant for the day. There is also much dancing and singing. The third day is elaborate with the peacock dance.

Omi

River Goddess Festival

The Osun Festival takes place in Nigeria in August of every year. It began in the 18th century and commemorates and renews the pact between the divine Goddess Osun and Oba (King) Laroye, the founder of Osogbo State, Nigeria. The pact ensured the Goddess will keep on protecting the people of the area as long as they continued to worship her. She is said to have immortalized the town Osogbo with her magical powers. Osun is a deeply revered Goddess of water, fertility, wealth, wisdom, art and diplomacy. She is seen as the Goddess of not just Nigeria but the universal Goddess of the whole of humanity.

Her festival is colorful and elaborate. It is a time when thousands from all over the world gather at her sacred historic river situated in the Sacred Grove of Osun now a world heritage site. Many individuals receive healing at this time.

Omi

Ganga Festival

The Ganga Festival in Varanasi is one of the most significant ceremonies held every year in India.

This famous festival is celebrated between the months of October and November. Dedicated to River Goddess Ganga the worship and seeking healing from her revered River Ganga is the main ritual. The festival renews and refreshes each individual's relationship with the river and the Goddess herself. The river is lit up by the devotional floating lamps set on its waterways. This spectacular festival is marked by an even more spectacular one dedicated to the Goddess- Dev Deepavali also known as the Festival of Lights.

Omi

Earth Reflection Notes

_____
_____
_____
_____
_____
_____
_____
_____
_____
_____
_____
_____
_____
_____
_____
_____
_____
_____
_____
_____
_____
_____
_____
_____
_____

Earth Reflection Notes

_____
_____
_____
_____
_____
_____
_____
_____
_____
_____
_____
_____
_____
_____
_____
_____
_____
_____
_____
_____
_____
_____
_____
_____

Earth Reflection Notes

Earth Reflection Notes

Earth

Earth

The fingers of winter caressed our faces. We stood there in the darkness on the even darker soil of the Catawba Indian Nation. The reservation was quiet as we bowed our heads in prayer. The immenseness of the night mingled with the flickering of five candles which had been lit and floated on water in the simple humble gesture of gratitude for life on Earth. We gave thanks for all that we had received from Mother Earth's waters and the world. We also asked for our own healing, It was January 2009, the first Humanity4Water water awareness and gratitude ceremony we conducted in South Carolina, United States.

Human history has been shaped from the richness of the Earth's crust. Half a million years ago we were in the throes of the Stone Age where the stones of the Earth shaped our existence. We then discovered that copper was easier to shape than stone taking us into the Copper Age. From the Copper Age we discovered how to separate iron from rock using heat heralding us into the Iron Age. From the 1750's we entered the Coal, Oil and Uranium Age. We have now near depleted the gifts provided by the sacred element of Earth.

There is very little that we receive that we don't get from the Earth: nourishment from the plants that grow towards the sun, oxygen from the outstretched trees and plant life that stretch elegantly upward toward the warm rays of the sun, a flourishing eco system, beauty that makes the eyes transfixed and the soul sing with joy.

The rainforest, the vital organs of the Earth keep us going. Once they were twice the size of Europe, now they have been halved. They covered 14% of the world's surface now they spread their glory on only 6%. They are: 70 million years old; home to half of the world's species of 10 million plants, animals and insects; contain libraries of biodiversity; provide medicine for the world. Currently 25 % of the world's pharmaceutical cures come from the rain forest.

The soil underneath the shade of the eye catching branches of the great rainforest trees is not fertile as nutrients have been leached away after long periods of time. Now many of the roots of these trees reach upward absorbing their nutrients from the sky. Yet, in our drive to whet the appetite of consumerism we clear these forest at 30 acres or more a minute. Much of the land is cleared to provide burgers for North Americans and for the profits of corporate companies.

The service of the rainforest, trees, animals, insects and plants that rise from the warmth of the soil is immense. Dig up one acre of soil beneath your feet and you may find bacteria, insects and soil life that is busy churning dead organic matter and waste into nutrients. You may well find: 50,000 small earthworms and their relatives, 50,000 insects and mites, nearly 12 million round worms, 30,000 protozoa, 50,000 algae, 400,000 fungi and billions of bacteria.

The soil itself does not stop yielding its service as it regulates our carbon, nitrogen and sulfur cycles and stores these contributions towards the warming of the planet deep in its robes.

These services and our relationship with the sacred element of Earth has always been honored in the dances of the Cherokee as they dance to the Corn and Harvest Moons, the Ghanaians colorful sacred acknowledgment of the harvest season, as the Hindus give time worn praise in the Pongal Harvest festival. As Susan Griffin, Philosopher and Poet eloquently stated,

we know ourselves to be made from this Earth.

We know this Earth is made from our bodies.

For we see ourselves. And we are nature. We are nature seeing nature. We are nature with a concept of nature. Nature speaking

of nature.

~ 149 ~

However the advance of consumerism which was and is wrapped up in the words "advancement of civilization" has seen us break and ignore the sacred pact man has always had with the Earth and Earth with man. This pact was treated as important to the survival of mankind and the whole of life by indigenous cultures across the corridors of the world. In the documentary "The Last Stand at Little Big Horn", which addressed some of the myths surrounding "Custer's Last Stand", Sitting Bull epitomized the attitude of the "sacred pact" when he would not sell The Sacred Black Mountains. Disgusted he thought "what price can you put on the Earth?" His disgust was echoed in his reply to the immigrant invaders who marched towards "progress", "we should take handfuls of earth and sell it by the pound."

Beautiful Blanket

The Earth is my blanket.

Native American saying.

Hindu Prayer, Shanti Path

"There is peace in Heavenly region; there is peace in the environment; the water is cooling; herbs are healing; the plants are peace-giving; there is harmony in the celestial objects and perfection in knowledge; everything in the universe is peaceful; peace pervades everywhere. May that peace come to me!"

This prayer is recited to conclude every Hindu ceremony, and to reflect the connectedness of humans with nature

Affirmation

Today I send love to the Earth.

A Gratitude Prayer for Mother Earth

Dear Mother Earth

Thank you for supporting my every step,

Thank you for your infinite wisdom,

Thank you for caring for me,

Even when I seem to

Not show you love back.

Dear Mother Earth,

I apologize for the love I have not

Shown you.

Today,

I embrace your wisdom,

Today I give my thanks,

Today I give my love.

I ask you Mother to keep

Me in your loving embrace,

From now until forever.

Thank you Great Mother Earth.

Omi

Gratitude to the Tree

Thank you mighty oak.
Thank you mighty willow.
Thank you mighty elm.
Thank you mighty pecan.
Thank you might orange.
Thank you mighty cedar.
Thank you mighty Pear.
Thank you mighty Breadfruit.
Thank you mighty pine.
Thank you mighty red heart.
Thank you to all the mighty trees
whose roots sustain the integrity
of this planet, the coolness
and freshness of water;
whose branches give shelter to all
Great Spirit's children;
whose fruits, barks and leaves
give us nourishment,
medicine and healing;
whose breath gives us life.
Thank you for all you do for me.
Thank you for all that you do for us.

Omi

The Wisdom of Trees

The trees are the keepers of wisdom.

They are where the ancestors reside.

When there are no more trees

There is no more wisdom left in the world.

Native American, Spirit Guide

Celebrate

June 5th

World Environmental Day

World Environment Day, commemorated each year on
5 June, is one of the principal vehicles through which the
United Nations stimulates worldwide awareness of the
environment and enhances political attention and action.

Sowing the Seeds Ceremony

Honor the Earth by keeping all the seeds from the fruit
you eat

and scatter those seeds in the woods.

Those seeds add to our eco-system

and bear us wisdom, nourishment

and love.

*Chief Randall of Little Horse Creek shares how to give back to
the Earth*

Everything Has Purpose

Everything on the Earth has a purpose, every disease a
herb to cure it, and every person a mission. This is the
Indian theory of existence.

Mourning Dove (Salish) 1888-1936

Earth in Balance

The climate crisis brings us the opportunity to experience what few generations in history have had the privilege of knowing: a generational mission, the exhilaration of a compelling moral purpose, a shared and unifying cause, and the thrill of being forced by circumstances to put aside the pettiness and conflict that so often stifle the restless human need for transcendence.

Al Gore, Earth in Balance

We are Part of the Soil

The American Indian is of the soil, whether it be the region of forests, plains, pueblos, or mesas. He fits into the landscape, for the hand that fashioned the continent also fashioned the man for his surroundings. He once grew as naturally as the wild sunflowers; he belongs just as the buffalo belonged.

Luther Standing Bear Oglala Sioux, 1868-1937

I dreamt of Trees Dying

Dear Great wise one,

I dreamt you were dying.

I dreamt that your branches were wilting.

I dreamt that your roots were rotting.

I dreamt that you were diseased.

I dreamt that your pain was calling me.

I dreamt that without you the water

is no more.

Without you the Earth is no more.

Without you the birds are no more.

Without you the insects are no more.

Without you the clean air is no more.

Without you wisdom will die.

Omi

Celebrate

June 8th

World Ocean Day

World Ocean was first proposed in 1992 by the Government of Canada at the Earth Summit in Rio de Janeiro. Although not yet officially designated by the United Nations, an increasing number of countries mark June 8th as an opportunity each year to celebrate our world ocean and our personal connection to the sea.

Affirmation

Today I go beyond limitations.

A contract with Earth

Treat the Earth well.
It was not given to you by your parents,
it was loaned to you by your children.
We do not inherit the Earth from our Ancestors,
we borrow it from our children.

Ancient Indian Proverb

Sacredness of Life

The sacred Rig Veda text of India regarded trees and plants as possessing divine healing properties, and it is still popularly believed that every tree has a Vriksa-devata, a tree deity. They are ritually worshiped with prayer, offerings, and the sacred thread ceremony. The Vriksa-devatas are not worshiped as gods, but as manifestations of the Divine. Tree planting is considered a religious duty.

Omi

Celebrate

June 17th

World Day for Combating Desertification and Drought

This day highlights the problems of millions who live in dry land regions. Desertification is not the advance of deserts; it is the process of land degradation which is often the result of human activity. So it can be controlled with our efforts. Rising temperatures in Africa are already exacerbating the problem and threatening to make it much worse.

Hugging the Trees

In March of 1973 in Gopeshwar, India, villagers formed a human chain and hugged trees marked to be cut down for the development of a sports equipment factory. This courageous action helped to spark a great ecological movement the Chipko Andolan (movement to hug trees).

Omi

The Secret Hug

You use to tell me that you gained strength from the trees.
You told me about the hugs you would give them
on your early morning walks,
long before the talks,
you know the ones.
The ones of the globe heating up.
You told me that I should try it too.
I found the thought amusing,
But the action way too embarrassing.
"Surely people would think I am crazy,"
I use to tell you.
Just recently, well ten years recently,
I walked past a pine forest with my husband.
Drawn by its perfume and beauty,
I walked amongst its elegance,
then I found myself hugging not one but two trees.
Can I tell you a secret?
It felt so good.
My feet felt like the roots that home
themselves in the ground.
Okay, one more secret I would like to share.
I did keep on looking over my shoulder as I enjoyed my tree
hug.
Hopefully next time I won't care.

Omi

~ 169 ~

Affirmation

Today I create a bright future for myself
and others.

Plant a Tree

Help repopulate our dying tree population. By supporting
organizations such as The Tree people at
www.treepeople.org.

Celebrate
Every 22nd of each month

Mother of the Earth Day

Started by Humanity4Water founders Derrick Lewis and
Omileye Achikeobi – Lewis, Mother of the Earth day
empowers each person with the knowledge small
contributions really do make a difference to our planet.
Individuals are encouraged to do something positive for
Mother Earth and humanity, once a month. Find out more
by visiting www.yeyeosun.com

Egyptian Soil

Egyptian irrigators did not experience many of the vexing problems that plagued (other historic) irrigation societies. The single season of planting did not overly deplete the soil, and fertility was naturally restored each year by the return of the silt-laden flood waters. In some basins, farmers planted grains and nitrogen-fixing legumes in alternative years, which helped maintain the soil's productivity. Fallowing land every other year, which was essential in (areas like) Mesopotamia, was thus unnecessary in the Nile valley.

Sandra Postal, Pillars of Sand

Tree Gratitude and Healing

When I tried hugging a tree, it felt so good. At first I thought it was a crazy idea but the ancients did it all the time. It is a great way of re-energizing.

Just pick a tree you feel drawn to,

and give it a big hug.

Feel its energy, give gratitude

for all that it does for us and ask permission

to receive healing from it.

Spend at least five to ten minutes in your tree embrace.

Omi

The Importance of Tree Planting and its Protection

Finally, I would like to make a suggestion regarding the use of your farmland in the settlement. In this settlement you have already initiated a project of planting fruit trees on farmlands. I think it is a very good plan. By planting fruit trees on your land we can not only ensure that the farmland remains productive, but also you will have fruits to eat. In short, I would like to again emphasize that it is extremely important to plant new trees and protect the ones already growing around you.

Extract of Speech of His Holiness The Dalai Lama on December 6, J 990, at a special ceremony held in Doeguling Tibetan Settlement, Mundgod, South India. Adapted from Appropriate Technology for Tibetan's (ApTibet) Newsletter No.5, September 1991

The Importance of Trees

It is said trees are the largest and longest living organisms on Earth. To grow tall the tree is almost a miracle of ecological engineering A tree is able to take water and salts out of the earth and lift them up to the leaves, sometimes over 400 ft above. By means of photosynthesis the leaves combine the water and salts with carbon dioxide from the air to produce the nutrients, which feed the tree. In this process, as well as wood, trees create many chemicals, seeds and fruit of great utility to man. Trees also remove carbon dioxide, the main greenhouse gas, from the air.

Tropical rain forests are of great significance; currently they occupy less than 6 per cent of the land surface of the Earth but are responsible for sustaining more than half of the biological species on the planet. They also keep our waterways cool and help to sustain the life connected with it.

Omi- The Green party expressed shock and concern at satellite pictures which reveal the destruction of the Amazon Rainforest has been estimated by as much as 60%

Trees are Sacred to us

The town in which I live is called Manistee, the name in
Indian language means spirit of the woods. This was a
place in which the Indians used to come to seek spiritual
visions. The spirit of the woods name came from the
Indians that used to make their way up the river and the
conifers would speak to them when the wind blew
through the limbs and foliage, thus the name.

*Don, Native American answering a question from an enquirer at
AllExperts.com who wanted to know about the significance of
trees in Native American culture*

Be Still Like the Earth

All the things that are still and move slowly like the trees
and the Earth live the longest.

Be like the tree and be like the Earth.

Omi, 2009

Celebrate

July 11th

World Population Day

In 1968, world leaders proclaimed that individuals have a basic human right to determine freely and responsibly the number and timing of their children. Forty years later, modern contraception remains out of reach for hundreds of millions of women, men and young people.

Trees Talking

My father always told me that the trees talk.

I use to say, "okay dad". He used to say, "no really, it's true."

Then one day I began to notice the sounds of each tree and the noise it makes as it sways.

I began to notice how

Each tree bent to the wind,

and even the shape of each tree tells you a story.

Cindy Canti, Native American

Affirmation

Today I commit to action.

Balancing the Earth

The Four Directions, which occur either literally or in symbolic form throughout the stories. These are often represented by particular colours, or by animals.

The Four Directions have to be in balance for all to be well with the world, and often a central point of balance is identified as a fifth direction; for example, four brothers represent the outer directions, and their sister the centre.

Many traditional cultures: African, Chinese, Native American, Buddhist, Indian believe that it is important to acknowledge each of the four corners of the Earth which represent all the elements of the universe and balance.

Adapted from Wikipedia

The Speed of Global Warming

The latest from the scientific community is that since 2000, emissions from burning fossil fuels have significantly outpaced the estimates used in 2007 climate study reports, and the pace of global warming has increased much more than predicted.

Omi

Melting Earth

Dear Mother Earth they say your ice is melting faster than expected.

They say you are shifting underneath our feet. They say that that the more your ice melts

the more your sea levels rise,

and the more millions of people will

suffer, your animals will suffer, your birds will suffer, your trees will suffer.

The oceans will be diluted

changing your salinity.

You know what that means Mother?

Your fish will be hurt, your polar bears too,

and there will be nothing to reflect your sunlight anymore.

Scientists now estimate the melting of Antarctica's massive ice sheets will cause the world's sea levels to rise by 1-2 meters by the end of the century.

Omi

More Ice Information

Antarctica is a continent of ice. This mass of ice binds the continent. If the ice continues to melt, Antarctica would be a small continent (eastern Antarctica) and a string of islands where the Antarctic Peninsula is located. This huge ice sheet has a big effect on the Earth's weather, reflecting great amounts of heat from the sun back into the atmosphere, tying up large amounts of Earth's freshwater, and acting as a freezer at the end of the Earth.

Since 1979 the ice of the Antarctic has shrunk by over 20% . The Polar bears are the most obvious animals suffering from this situation. The habitat of the polar bears is the ice flow areas around the edges of the caps. As the caps melt, the flows are disappearing and pulling back to the extent that there is no ice on the shores. The extent of the melting is such that a Russian ship was able to reach the North Pole in 2005 without the use of an ice breaker. This lost habitat is pushing the polar bears to the edge of extinction. Various estimates put the total population at 20,000 and dropping.

Omi

The Circle of Life

Life is a circle. The world is a circle. The Christian way of seeing the world is that within this circle there's a man called Jesus; on the outside is the trees, the rocks, the animals; all around the world are the different things that are on Mother Earth. In the center is man above all things.

The Indian way of thinking is that there is this same circle, Mother Earth and around her are the rocks, the trees, the grass, the mountains, the birds, the four-legged, and man. Man is the same as all those other things, no greater, no less.

Mark St Pierre and Tilda Long Soldier, Walking in the Sacred Manner

Affirmation

Today I give thanks.

We Are One

If more people looked beyond themselves,

they would realize that everything in life

is interconnected.

I think if more people did this there would be

less selfishness.

Rudy Mancke, South Carolinian Naturalist

Coming Together

It is possible that we have been brought together at this
time because we have profound truths to teach each other.
From an indigenous perspective, the individual psyche can
be healed only by addressing one's relationships with the
visible worlds of nature and community and one's
relationships with the invisible forces of the ancestors and
Spirit allies.

Malidoma Patrice Some, author of Of Water and the Spirit

Earth, Balance and Ceremonies

The Dogon perform rituals to restore, maintain, or vitalize
the balance of supernatural forces and the human
community. They believe that all these super naturals
contribute to the spiritual well-being and order of the
human community. The loss of contact and control of any
of these super naturals results in a state of disorder or
spiritual imbalance which the Dogon call puru or death.
The goal of any ritual is to regain this spirit loss and
restore order to the balance of the supernatural world, and
thus to the human community. This results in the state
which the Dogon call omo or living.

DeMott, Dogon Masks . (the Dogons are from West Africa)

Gently, But With Purpose

Tread this Earth gently, but with purpose.

Treat all that you meet along the way with gentleness and
they will sway, curl and unfold as if doing the dance of
nature.

Smiles become like rose petals kissed by the morning dew.

Tread gently on the Earth, but with purpose. Purpose of
your destiny, always towards your destiny, but, tread
gently on the Earth.

Remah Joseph

Honey Dance

They tell me the dance that you do,
the enticing dance of honey,
the dance that brings sweetness to my lips,
the dance that shows collective steps
are more powerful than a single one
the dance that celebrates the coming home of a full sac of
honey into your nest,
the dance that tells all that Great Spirits sweetness is
nearby, the dance where you wag and show off those
skills, the dance that has kept humanity fascinated
since the beginning of time, the dance that keeps us fed ,
the dance that sustains all Mother Earth's children, will
soon be no more.

Omi

*In honor of the Honey Bee which is fast disappearing. The
majority of wild pollinators have now disappeared from the
Earth as a result of humans destroying their habitats.*

*The honey bee has now taken over as the main pollinator. It
pollinates most of the wild plants and one fourth of crops in the
United States alone and countries worldwide. Many Scientist
have said the disappearance of our honey bees will result in
widespread starvation.*

Celebrate

August 9th

International Day for World Indigenous People

On 23 December 1994, the General Assembly decided that the International Day of the World's Indigenous People shall be observed on 9 August every year during the International Decade of the World's Indigenous People.

Disappearing Honey Bees

Honeybees are vanishing at an alarming rate from 24 US states, threatening the production of numerous crops.

The cause of the losses, which range from 30% to more than 70%, is a mystery, but experts are investigating several theories.

Bees pollinate more than $14bn (£7bn) worth of US seeds and crops each year, mostly fruits, vegetables and nuts.

The mysterious disappearances highlight the important link that honeybees play in the chain that brings fruit and vegetables to supermarkets and dinner tables.

BBC News, February 2007," Bee vanishing act baffles keepers ".

Affirmation

Today I greet the whole world with a
smile.

Back to the Sacred

I believe that our people, and all people all over this Earth,
are going back. They are already searching for something;
they don't know what it is they are going back to. It's the
creator.

Jackie Yellow Tale Crow, Traveler on the Sacred walk

The Animals Know

If you want to know if something is going to happen

watch the animals.

If the animals go to the mountains,

you better go too because something

is about to happen.

Beckee Garris, Catawba Medicine Woman, 2009

Bengal Tiger Grace

Oh, striped one
I saw you, on that show.
Big, tall, and proud.
you moved with such elegance,
such grace.
You show of the hand of God
That makes everything so well.
then I saw the documentary,
how the villagers feared your every mood.
They said you were ferocious and a man killer.
They said you eat their livestock,
They said you prowled by night and made them scared.
Then I saw the blood. I am sorry I had to see it,
one thousand people bludgeoned you to death.
Your only crime – being a youngster lost.
Now I have to face the truth that
Your graceful ways are no longer seen
but sensed with fear.
We no longer see the beauty of what
Great Spirit has made.
Like so many other things,
we have not reconciled,
we are part of you and you us.

Omi

~ 198 ~

Adopt a Tiger

On average the Bengal tigers measure s three meters from head to tail. The males are often bigger than the females. A male Bengal tiger can weight 220kg, or 34 stone, and have a territory of up to 100 square km.

Bengal tigers are the subspecies that produce the famous white tigers. The majority of Bengal tigers are found in India, although some prefer neighboring countries such as Nepal. They are extremely adaptable as to their habitats, which range from the hot jungles of North India to the icy forests of the Himalayas.

Sadly, the number of Bengal tigers is at an all-time low. It is estimated that they vary in numbers from 3000 to 4500 (at the time of writing) with around 300 in captivity - and they are still on the decline.

Tigers in general are on the decline with three of the original 8 sub species of tigers being extinct. The biggest threat to tigers is de-forestation which destroys their habitat and leaves them with no food. The clearing away of land for farming also leaves tigers in danger from farmers who will shoot them on sight in order to protect their livestock. Their pelts are highly valuable and make them subject to poaching.

There are many schemes dedicated to the protection of tigers. Adopting a tiger, joining a charity and/writing letters to the relevant government officials are very effective ways to helping tigers from going into complete extinction. Remember there are many animals facing the same dilemmas. Any help you give will make a huge difference to our planet.

Omi (*Adapted from Wikipedia and www.bangalinet.com*)

Affirmation

Today I admire the beauty of life.

Healing the Spirit of Horses

I played a healing flute to the horses.

One of the horses stood there for a long time,

with its ears perked up.

It brought its face so close to the flute,

I could feel its spirit,

I could sense its gratitude,

I heard the words,

"thank you for giving something back to us".

Omi on her experience of playing the healing flute to horses in South Carolina. She believes that horses hold an important message of healing to the world. She would like to say thank you to Katie Holme from Healing Horses for the work she does.

Adopt a Horse

Help an abused horse rehabilitate and have a better home.
Find out how supporting Healing Horses at
www.healinghorses.us.

Listen to the Animals Meditation

Take a moment out of your time to observe
the animals.

Still your thoughts and focus in on your feelings,

observe the animals' movements, sounds, actions, and
colors.

What can you learn about the animal or animals you
observed?

The more you repeat this exercise the more you will learn.

Omi

Earth Meditation for Healing

Earth is the element that relates to your base chakra, or energy center.

It relates to the ability to be dynamic, purposeful, ambitious, grounded, energized, and full of vision.

When this energy center is impaired you will feel none of the above. You will feel fearful, disorientated, not grounded, a lack of energy and direction. You can re-balance your earth energy center.

Find a quiet space, gently inhale and exhale.

On each inhalation breathe in the grounding color red.

On each exhalation release all your tension.

As your body relaxes, imagine roots of energy extending from your feet and sinking into the ground, helping you feel more grounded and re-energized.

Omi

Earth Meditation Our Children

Close your eyes inhale and exhale gently.

Feel your whole body relax.

You are in a magic forest.

The magic forest is very beautiful;

It is warm and sunny.

You meet many interesting and magical creatures;

see many interesting things.

Explore and enjoy your adventures.

After you have had some fun in the forest,

wave goodbye to all your new friends,

and tell yourself you will never forget the magic

and freedom of the forest.

Slowly stretch and open your eyes when you have
finished.

Omi

Affirmation

Today I heal Mother Earth.

The Green Corn Dance

The Green Corn Dance is done a few weeks before the corn is ripe. The ceremony is an annual rite of renewal and purification. It was dedicated to the Gods who controlled the growth of corn or maize.

It was considered a crime to even touch the ripened corn before the Green Corn Dance.

During the 18th century Indians of the South considered this as a time when they received new clothes, new pots and other household items. They would collect their old clothes, grains and household items, put them in a huge pile and then set them alight.

Omi

Adapted from various sources including:

www.meredity.edu/nativeam/green_corn_dance

The Powamu Festival

The Powamu Festival is a mid-winter ceremony. It is also called the Bean Planting Festival. The festival is observed in late January or early February. It is an 8 day Hopi Indian celebration

The Hopis believe that for 6 months of the year the ancestral spirits called Katchinas leave their mountain homes and visit the tribe. When they do this, they bring along with them good health for humans and rain for the crops. The Powamu Festival celebrates the return of these spirits.

The ceremony includes:

Repainting the mask that the Hopis wear to impersonate the Katchinas.

On the third day the men bring baskets of wet sand that they leave at the entrance of the Kiva (ceremonial meeting room).

A fire burns in the Kiva of every Hopi village for 8 days.

Blankets are stretched across the opening of the Kiva to make it like a hot house.

Each man who enters the Kiva during this period carries a basket or bowl of sand into it. He also plants a handful of beans, which sprout because of the heat inside.

The ceremony concludes with a dance that takes place in the nine kivas that dot the northeastern Arizona mesa. This dance is done into the wee hours of the night.

In the morning the Katchinas arrive, wearing masks and with their bodies painted. They bring goodies for the boys and girls, who also receive the green bean sprouts that have been growing in the hot Kiva. Then a big feast is had by all with the bean sprouts forming a large part of the menu.

Adapted from Holidays, Symbols & Customs
by Sue Ellen Thomas

We Do Not Own the Water

If we do not own the freshness of the air and the sparkle of the water, how can you buy them?

Chief Seattle, Chief of the Suquamis

The Ongkor Festival

The Ongkor Festival is an ancient festival held in August in farming areas of Tibet. It celebrates the time when the crops are ready for harvesting.

"Ongkor" in Tibetan means "surrounding the farmland." Major activities include: horse racing, shooting, singing and dancing, Tibetan Opera, stone holding and wrestling.

The Ongkor Festival

originated in the historic valley at the middle and lower reaches of the Yarlung Zangbo River.

The Zetang in the Sharman Region of Tibet holds the Ongkor Festival in mid-summer. Each family sends out a representative, mostly women, to form a 100-member team. They dress in grand Tibetan robes, wear their gold and silver jewels, carry dou (a measuring instrument for grain) and scripture book, colurful arrows, produce from their farms. Under the leadership of a revered man and accompanied by the sounds of ritual trumpets and drums, they move round the farmland outside the village, shouting: "Yangguxiu! Yangguxiu!" (meaning "Come back, the soul of the Earth!").

Omi

Celebrate

September 16th

International Day for Preserving the Ozone Layer

On 19 December 1994, the United Nations General Assembly proclaimed 16 September the International Day for the Preservation of the Ozone Layer, commemorating the date, in 1987, on which the Montreal Protocol on Substances that Deplete the Ozone Layer was signed.

The Pongal Harvest Festival

The spirit of Pongal, the harvest festival of Tamil Nadu in
India, is one of thanksgiving to God for a bountiful
harvest. It is a three-day festival that is celebrated on
January 14th. It is one of the few Dravidian festivals that
have survived the Indo-Aryan influences. Pongal also
marks the beginning of the New Year and is the day to
praise and thank God with full devotion, faith and
sincerity of heart. Old vices and past habits are abandoned
forever on this day. All things are honored on this day.
Even the insects are not overlooked and are offered rice
flour to feed on in the form of 'Kollam' at the entrance way
of every house. Pongal is seen as a day for peace and
happiness for all.

Omi

The Origins of Pongal

Once upon a time the first day of the festival Pongal was once dedicated to Lord Indra. The young child Krishna, who is traditionally seen as the personification of the Supreme Being felt that Indra was very arrogant so he decided to teach Indra a big lesson. When the Pongal festival was due Krishna's father and those who were cow herders began to prepare for it including getting ready their offerings for Indra.

Krishna objected and persuaded them to worship Mount Govardhan instead. . When Indra found out what Krishna and the villagers had been up to he was furious, so furious he sent thunderous pours, storms and lightning to drown and punish them. The fierce rains sent by Indra continued for three days creating much devastation in its wake. When Indra saw what he had done. He begged Krishna's Krishna's forgiveness. Krishna accepted and allowed the Pongal celebrations to continue in honor of Indra.

__Omi's__ version of traditional story of the origins of the Pongal festival

The Earth and Us

They have surrounded me and left me nothing more
than an island. When we had the land we were strong.
Now we are melting like snow on the hillside.

Red Cloud, Lakota Leader

Homowo Yam Festival

Throughout Western Africa there are various Yam Festivals held annually usually in August or September. This is a time when the rainy season is coming to an end and crops are ripe for harvest. There is plenty of corn as well as other vegetables. Yam is a common, versatile and important part of the staple diet. They can be cooked in many ways: roasted, boiled, and added to soups, stews, fried, mashed, dried or pounded into flour.

The Yam Festival in Ghana, a country in western Africa, is also called the "Homowo" or "To Hoot at Hunger" Festival. It is a time when the people hope for a good harvest so that no famine will hit the people in the coming year. In Nigeria, also in western Africa, the Yam festival is called "Iriji" which means "New Yams". The people also hope for a plentiful harvest. In Nigeria, the festival is celebrated mainly by the Igbo people. Other communities celebrate it too. Each community celebrates Iriji in different ways. But, all have a parade, songs, dancing and drumming. Because a good yam harvest is important for survival, the people give thanks to the spirits of the Earth and sky.

In Ghana the "To Hoot at Hunger Festiva" takes place in many rural communities. It is a lot of fun as women dig up the yams and carry them home in baskets on their heads.

~ 217 ~

Everyone is trying to be the family with the largest crop. Villagers gather together as the women and young girls prepare the feast, with the yams as prized food. A young boy is chosen to carry the best yams to the festival dinner, and another boy follows him beating a drum. Other young people from the village march to the beat of the drum and the sound of a woodwind instrument, and sometimes musket fire. Chiefs make a procession under huge umbrellas and wearing robes made from the traditional bright colored, Ghanaian Kente Cloth. They follow the yams, and the young people dance. Other activities include singing, wearing animal masks, and displaying traditional items to the spirits and ancestors.

Omi

Affirmation

Today I celebrate life.

The Kwatuitl Winter Ceremony

For Reconnection

The Kwatuitl Native Indians inhabit the Pacific North West, Alaska and part of the Vancouver Island in British Colombia.

They believed that in the beginning the world was ruled by animals and insects which had super natural powers which they generously shared with some human beings. These humans became the ancestors of the Kwatuitl.

The Kwatuitl Winter Ceremony happens in mid-winter. It acknowledges and re-affirms the Kwatuitl's relationship with the natural world.

They perform dances including the Hamatsa dance which is performed by men dressed in strips of cedar bark and wearing ornately decorated mask designed in such a way as to invoke the spiritual essence of nature and their ancestors.

The ceremony includes a great feast at which salmon is always served.

Omi

~ 220 ~

Yam Festival Muffins

INGREDIENTS

1 cup cooked yams, mashed
1 3/4 cups all-purpose flour
1/2 teaspoon salt
1/2 cup sugar
2 teaspoons baking powder
2 eggs
4 tablespoons, sweet butter, melted
3/4 cup milk
1 teaspoon cinnamon

METHOD

1. Preheat oven to 350 degrees F (175 degrees C), and grease muffin tins, or arrange paper muffin cups on a baking sheet.

2. In a large mixing bowl, combine all ingredients and mix well

3. Pour the batter into the muffin tins or paper cups until 2/3 full and bake

Omi

Delicious Yam Festival Brownies

INGREDIENTS

Golden Yam Brownies

1 cup butter

1 cup packed brown sugar

4 eggs

2 teaspoons vanilla extract

1 ½ cups all purpose flour

1 teaspoon baking powder

½ teaspoon salt

2 cups peeled and finely shredded yam

1 cup confectioner's sugar

2 tablespoons butter or margarine

2 tablespoons of milk

DIRECTIONS

1. Preheat the oven to 350° F (175° C)

2. Grease a 9 x 12 inch baking dish

3. In a large bowl, cream together the butter, brown sugar and white sugar until smooth. Beat in the eggs, and then stir in the vanilla. Combine the flour, baking powder and salt; stir into the batter just until blended. Fold in the shredded yam; spread the batter evenly in the greased baking dish

4. Bake for 30 minutes in the preheated oven.

5. Mix together the confectioners. sugar, butter and milk until smooth. Spread over the brownies while they are still warm.

6. Serve hot.

Omi

Celebrate

World Monitor Day

September 18th

World Water Monitoring Day™ is an international
education and outreach program that builds public
awareness and involvement in protecting water resources
around the world by engaging citizens to conduct basic
monitoring of their local water bodies.

Do Not Destroy Your Home

The frog does not drink up the pond
in which he lives.

Native American Proverb

Pongal Festival Lemon Rice Recipe

Ingredients:
2 cup Basmati rice,
1 tsp Channa dal,
1 tsp Urad dal,
1/4 tsp asafoetida (heeng),
1/4 tsp mustard seeds,
1/4 tsp turmeric powder,
2 tsp Ghee,
Juice of 2 lemons, and
Salt to taste.

Method:
1. Wash and clean the rice thoroughly.
2. Boil it in 1/4 litre of water till done.
3. Heat the Ghee in a separate shallow pan.
4. Add mustard seeds, channa dal, Urad dal, asafoetida and turmeric powder to it.
5. Fry lightly till it emits fragrance.
6. Mix well with cooked rice for flavor.
7. Add salt to the lemon juice and pour it over rice and mix well.

Omi

Pongal Festival Recipe

Ingredients:
1 finely-grated coconut,
1 tsp roasted Channa dal,
1 tsp roasted Urad dal,
1/4 tsp asafoetida (heeng),
2 green chilies,
1/4 tsp turmeric powder,
Assortment of vegetables, excluding salad and leafy
vegetables and beetroot (cut and diced).

Method:
1. Blanch the diced vegetables and set it aside for later use.
2. Grind channa dal, Urad dal, asafoetida and green chillies to a paste.
3. Heat ghee in a separate shallow pan and add the grounded paste.
4. Fry lightly till it emits fragrance.
5. Add the grated coconut and sauté it over a low flame.
6. Add the blanched vegetables and cook till done.
7. Add salt to taste.

Omi

~ 227 ~

Pongal Festival Coconut Rice Recipe

Ingredients:

2 cups Raw Rice

Curry leaves a sprig

Asafoetida a pinch

3 Red chillies

4 or 5 tea spoons Mustard Oil

1 teaspoon Urad Dal

1 teaspoon Channa Dal

Salt to taste

1 to 2 glass Water

Tamarind a small lime size

Method:

1. Soak rice for an hour, half dry in a towel and grind it
2. Heat oil in a pan; add mustard, after sizzling add red chillies, curry leaves, asafoetida, channa dal, Urad dal and salt.
3. Mix the tamarind with water a little concentrated.
4. Add it to the pan and add ground rice and fry.
5. Add more water, mix and close with lid.
6. Open then and there to cup if the rice is cooked, and add water accordingly.

7. The bottom will become dark brown and crisp. Remove from fire and serve with pickle or hot chutney -

Omi

The Kwatuitl Winter Ceremony Salmon Ashe

Ingredients - serves 4
4 x 175g/6oz salmon steaks or salmon fillets
soy sauce
2 cloves of garlic
2 tablespoons of barbecue sauce
2 teaspoons of black pepper
1 teaspoon of chicken seasoning stock
tablesp of olive oil
50g/2oz unsalted butter
50g/2oz fresh breadcrumbs
1 teasp grated lemon rind
1 teasp mixed herbs (see note*)

Method

1. Preheat the oven to 375F/190C/gas.
2. Mix the herbs with the breadcrumbs and lemon rind, season with salt & pepper.
3. Season the salmon with crushed garlic, soy sauce, barbecue sauce, black pepper, hot pepper sauce, chicken stock and olive oil. Leave to marinade for 1 hour.
4. Place salmon steaks in a greased, oven proof dish

5. Melt the butter and brush over the top of the salmon steaks. Spread the breadcrumb mixture over the top of the salmon steaks, and bake the salmon for 15 –20 minutes

Omi

Do a Harvest or Reconnection Festival

Do a harvest/reconnection festival with your family or

Community to celebrate

the nourishment, connection and support

that Mother Earth gives.

Duplicate a festival you know about

or take elements from various harvest

festivals and make a great

one of your own.

Omi

Carbon Footprint

Carbon footprint is "the total set of GHG (greenhouse gas) emissions caused directly and indirectly by an individual, organization, event or product" (UK Carbon Trust 2008). An individual, nation or organization's carbon footprint is measured by undertaking a GHG emissions assessment. Once the size of a carbon footprint is known, a strategy can be devised to reduce it.

Carbon offsets, or the mitigation of carbon emissions through the development of alternative projects such as solar or wind energy or reforestation, represent one way of managing a carbon footprint.

The concept and name of the carbon footprint originates from the ecological footprint discussion. The carbon footprint is a subset of the ecological footprint.

Omi. Check out the carbon calculator

on www.climatecrisis.net

How Big Is Your Carbon Footprint?

Before you can reduce it, you need to know how big it is. The average person in the UK alone causes the emission of 13,000kg of carbon dioxide equivalent gases per year. The global average is 5,800kg, in India it's around 1,300kg.

There are various ways of measuring your carbon footprint. Usually they're made up of a series of scores, such as Transport score, Energy score, Food score, and Waste.

Omi. Check out the carbon calculator

on www.climatecrisis.net and www.carbonfootprint.com

Ten and More Tips on Going Green

1. Buy less.

2. Do you really have to keep on shopping?! Reduce the demand on materials, resources and manufacturing.

3. Waste less.

4. Recycle, recycle, recycle. Do what you can to recycle, compost, repair, renovate, recondition and reuse.

5. Be smarter with your energy use.

6. What can you do to prevent heat loss, reduce energy use and convert to renewable energy systems?

7. Cut out the Synthetics.

8. Petroleum based materials such as conventional paint, stain, varnish, carpet, soft furnishings, textiles, sealant, glue, plastic, furniture, MFC, MDF, electrical equipment casing etc. Production uses large amounts of energy, creates toxic waste and once the materials are in your home this adds to indoor air pollution, causing a hazard to your health.

9. Be home conscious.

10. Try and think about the materials and products you are filling your home with. Ensure they don't have a high impact on the natural environment. Do some research before you buy and make informed decisions! Go for all things sustainable, renewable, natural, biodegradable, energy efficient, recycled, repaired and locally made.

11. Smart lighting.

12. Get smart with your lighting. Use clever interior design tips and ideas to make the most out of natural daylight. Look into Solar. Save electricity & money on your utility bill.

13. Buy locally.

14. Cut out shipping and transportation and opt for local manufacturers. Support the local economy and reduce the number of fossil fueled miles every time you shop local.

15. Add Something New.

16. Every month add a few things on to the list.

Omi

Fruit Offering

Do a fruit offering to the

Spirits and ancestors of the Earth.

Fill a basket up with your favorite fruit,

Place by a tree.

Take a few quiet moments to contemplate

And give thanks

to the nurturing energy of the

Earth.

Omi

Affirmation

All is good today.

Natural Healing

Visit a natural sight such as a forest, mud volcano, park,
and enjoy being with the power of nature.

Observe it,

feel it,

be with it.

Allow the energy of your being

and the energy of nature

to fill you up.

Omi

Earth Reflection Notes

Earth Reflection Notes

Earth Reflection Notes

_____
_____
_____
_____
_____
_____
_____
_____
_____
_____
_____
_____
_____
_____
_____
_____
_____
_____
_____
_____
_____
_____
_____
_____

Fire

~ 243 ~

Fire

14th March 2009, the sound of flutes raised rhythmically into the air, enfolding ethereal fingers with the spirit of water, earth, air and the sun. It was a dance so ancient that I stood there enraptured. Thirty Native Americans from a variety of nations swayed in time with the music as they offered up gratitude through prayers and song to the endless unconditional love and service of the sacred Healing Springs. A place which sprung from deep under the ground, connected to the long history of Blackville, South Carolina, and the Native Americans who healed families and wounded soldiers in its pristine pools.

This ceremony happened in the warmth and fire of the sun, in the same way much of life has emerged from the beginning of time. The gift of life is interesting and pressure. It springs from the wells of water and the ability of plant life capture the energy of the sun turning it into turning it into building blocks and sustenance.

The Egyptians, Mayans, Aztecs, Bushmen, Dogons, Celts, and Gallic all watched the immeasurable power of the sun rise and fall. Keeping a note of where it rose in the sky and where it set. They carved monuments, planted stones like at the famous Nabta site of Sub Saharan Africa (which is said to be older than Stone Hedge), did breathtaking cave paintings which tracked the path of the sun.

The honoring of the sun can be seen in the oldest form of the Goddess in Egypt who wore the sun on her head representing the timeless union between mankind and this sacred element. It can be seen every day when the thousands gather at the banks of the Ganges River in India and await the large warm face of the sun, meeting it with songs, cheers and prayers. Rightfully so. For we depend on this captivating star for the day, night, seasons, climates, food, warmth, oxygen we breathe (which is replenished by photosynthesis), light, and for making our planet hospitable and livable.

Formed 4.6 million years ago from the dust of one or more stars on the edge of our Milky Way galaxy the sun an ordinary star, is exceptional to us. As it lights up our whole world we may not think of the size of the sun. We get the true sense of its massiveness when we understand it is 93 million miles away from the Earth. It is 745 times more massive than all the planets combined.

The signature for precious elements that make up life can be seen in the light of the sun as German Chemist Gustav Kirchhoff, and coworker Robert Bunsen discovered in 1859 as they examined the flame of a Bunsen burner.

The sun and humans are made up of the same elements in the exact same quantity.

What is Life?

It is the flash of a firefly in the night.
It is the breath of a buffalo in the wintertime.
It is the little shadow which runs across
the grass and loses itself in the sunset.

Crowfoot, Blackfoot warrior and orator 1830 - 1890

Treat the Earth Well

It was not given to you by your parents;
it was loaned to you by your children.
We do not inherit the Earth from our Ancestors,
we borrow it from our Children.

Ancient Indian Proverb

Affirmation

Today as the planet heals, I heal too.

The Embrace of the Sun

The Earth has received the embrace of the sun and we shall
see the results of that love. He put in your heart certain
wishes and plans; in my heart, he put other different
desires.

Chief Sitting bull

Sun Gratitude Prayer

Dear Sun,

Thank you for your

energy,

light,

radiance,

heat,

warmth,

love,

life,

life force,

ever-presence.

Chief Awo Basorun,
Olu Derrick Lewis

~ 251 ~

Greeting the Sun Ritual

Do an ancient African ritual called
Greeting the Sun.
Wake up before sunrise.
Brush your teeth,
wash your face,
clean your ears,
and bathe in silence.
While you do this give thanks for everything
Great Spirit has given to you.
Give thanks for seeing another day.
Vow to use all your gifts wisely.
Step outside into your garden
or choose a room in your house
and give thanks to the four
corners of the Earth.
These four corners
represent the unity
and sustaining efforts of
the universe,
and the universal consciousness whose
rhythm we are all an integral part of.

Omi

The Inca Sun Festival

Among the four festivals which the Inca Kings celebrated in the city of Cuzco, the most solemn was that in honor of the Sun, during the month of June.

It was called Yntip Raymi, which means the "Solemn Feast of the Sun." The Festival of the Sun was the Incas way of showing their appreciation for all that the Sun did for the planet. They believed that the Sun represented the universal God who created and sustained all of life on Earth with his light and power. They saw him as the natural father of the first Inca. As a result this was one of their most serious festivals.

The festival was attended by anyone and everyone: chiefs, citizens and anyone who wanted to receive potent annual solstice blessings.

Omi

Affirmation

Today the planet is renewed and I am
renewed with it.

The Aztec Sun Stone Calendar

Many cultures arranged their days and festivals by the sun and moon. The famous Aztec sun calendar is one example of the ancients being in touch with the rhythm of nature.

The original calendar was actually a 25 ton 12 feet long stone slab carved in the 15th century. The calendar which was known as the Eagle Bowl was used for calculating auspicious days for religious, agricultural, and daily activities. It rounded the year into 365 days.

Omi

Gratitude to the Sun

Thank you for all the times
that you eased away my pain.
Thank you for all the times
you refreshed my mind.
Thank you for all the times
you made me feel hope again.
Thank you for all the moments
you embraced me.
Thank you for all the days
you greeted me.
Thank you for all the lives
you awaken with
your smile.
Thank you for nourishing the plants.
Thank you for loving the Earth.
Thank you for always making
each day better
for each of Mother Earth's children.

Om

Celebrate Summer Solstice

Late June is a time that traditionally marks the end of the year in many cultures. From time immemorial it was a time of great festivities and celebrations. A moment of thanks and to remember our relationship with Mother Earth. Just think of thousands flocking to the Ifa festival of West Africa where the wisdom of the ancient Oracle is called down or the equally famous Stonehenge Summer festival of the United Kingdom.

The Summer Solstice is a day when the sun appears at its greatest and the day is at its longest. The Winter Solstice occurs in late winter when the sun appears at its least. The other two seasons are fall and spring. These are marked by the equinoxes when the day and night are roughly equal.

Do your own special solstice celebration by having a special day of giving gratitude and holding a fun family discussion on how you can make a difference to the planet.

Omi

The Circle of Life

You have noticed that everything an Indian does is in a circle, and that is because the power of the world always works in circles, and everything tries to be round. The sky is round and I have heard that the Earth is round like a ball and so are all the stars. The wind, in its greatest power, whirls. Birds make their nests in circles for theirs is the same religion as ours. Even the seasons form a great circle in their changing and always come back again to where they were. The life of a man is a circle from childhood to childhood and so it is in everything where power moves.

Black Elk - Oglala Lakota

The Wisdom of Life

In the beginning of all things wisdom and knowledge were with the animals for Tirawa, the one above did not speak directly to man. He sent certain animals to tell men that he showed himself through the beasts and that from them and from the stars and the sun and the moon should man learn. All things tell of Tirawa.

Eagle Chief – Pawne

Sacred Rights

The Earth is the mother of all people, and all people should have equal rights upon it. You might as well expect the rivers to run backwards as that any man who was born a free man should be contented when penned up and denied liberty to go where he pleases.

Chief Joseph - Nez Perce

Celebrate

September 22nd

World Car Day

World Car free Day began as an open call for a grassroots celebration of cities without cars. The date, September 22, was chosen to coincide with the EU-sponsored European Mobility Week, but our hope is to involve people at all levels of society and from all over the world.

Affirmation

Today the creative energy of the
Universe flows through me.

The Sun Dance

The Sun Dance was the most important of all the ceremonies practiced by the Lakota and most of the Plains Indians. It was a time of renewal, both of the tribe and of the People and the Earth. As many tribes as possible would come together for this annual rite. At this time the village would be a hub of activity. A large circular arena would be cleared and a double ring of sticks would be erected around the outside with branches placed on the top as shelter for the dancers, singers and spectators. The Holy Men would go into the forest and select a tree to be used as the central pole. As it fell it was not allowed to touch the ground. The tree would then be trimmed, taken back to the dance site, decorated and erected in the middle of the arena

The dance would begin the next day at sunrise. Anyone who wanted to could do the dance. The dancers looked at the sun as they danced. Short breaks were allowed but no food or drink was taken. The sun dance was a time of purification and getting wishes granted. It was a great time of celebration.

Omi

~ 263 ~

The Ifa Festival

The Ifa Festival takes place at the beginning of June and culminates at the solstice. Amongst the Yoruba of Nigeria the solstice is seen as the beginning of the New Year and a time of renewal.

This festival is amongst the Yoruba's most sacred as it "brings down the Oracle" known as Ifa which represents the wisdom of God. It is attended by thousands of people from all over the Africa and the world. There are many days and weeks of prayers, chanting, and purification in order to bring the sacred Oracle down from Heaven to speak.

This ancient rite has been unbroken for thousands of year. By the end of the festival many priests gather together to interpret the messages from the Oracle. These messages predict what will happen for the world in that year.

For those who attend this festival it is a time to hear the universal world reading first hand and to receive their personal blessings for the year. The sacred messages received are very accurate.

Omi – who has experienced this festival twice.

How the Sun Became Respected

One day the divine being Iwori Meji made divination for the sun,

the Moon and Darkness when they were coming to the world.

In Yoruba they are called Djo for Sun, DShukpa for Moon and Dkuku for Darkness.

He advised the three brothers to make sacrifice as follows:-

SUN- to make sacrifice with a bundle of brooms, white cloth, white cock and a white hen.

MOON- to make sacrifice with red Cloth, a brown cock and a brown hen.

DARKNESS- to make sacrifice with black cloth, a black cock and a black hen.

He advised them to make the sacrifice so that the people of the world might honour and respect them, but more especially so that people might not look contemptuously at them on the face.

More importantly, the sacrifice was meant to give them power and energy which would make them indispensable, wherever they went.

The moon said that he was too handsome and popular to worry about any sacrifice. The Darkness said he

was already endowed with adequate features to command respect and fear anywhere he went. He too refused to make any sacrifice.

The Sun was the only one who made a sacrifice. The Moon had however earlier made sacrifice for love which is why people rejoice at the sight of the new moon.

After his sacrifice, the Sun was given the bundle of brooms (with which he made his sacrifice with) to hold in his hand always. He was advised that he should point the broom at the face of anyone who dared to stare at him on the face. To this day that broom is the rays of the sun which dazzles the eyes of anyone who tries to look directly at the face of the Sun. He is nonetheless admired, because the heat he generates is used for a variety of purposes throughout the planetary system.

No one cares very much about darkness and it is not used for any tangible purpose because he made no sacrifice. For the same reason, the moon is merely admired but is neither dreaded like the sun, nor used for any productive purpose.

Omi. Adapted from the ancient Yoruba sacred text on how the sun became respected. The story warns against arrogance.

~ 266 ~

Celebrate

All October

International Walk to School Month

International Walk to School Month gives children, parents, school teachers and community leaders an opportunity to be part of a global event as they celebrate the many benefits of walking.

Dinewan, Brolga and How the Sun Was Created

Once upon a time there was no sun and no humans. The planet was inhabited by only birds, beasts, the moon and stars.

The animals of those times were much larger than their cousins of today. One day Dinewan the emu and Brolga his companion quarreled and fought. Dinewan made Brolga so angry she rushed to his nest, seized and grabbed a huge precious egg. With all her anger and force she threw it up to the sky. The egg broke on a bundle of firewood. The firewood burst into flames, the yellow yolk spilled all over it making the flame get so big it lit up the whole world below. The creatures on Earth were astonished. They had never seen so much light. They had been living in darkness all that time.

One of the good sky spirit noticed how beautiful and bright the Earth looked when lit up by the fires light. He thought it would be a wonderful idea to make a fire every day. So one night he and his attendants began to collect, and heap up firewood. When the heap was big enough they sent out the morning star to warn those on Earth the fire will soon be lit. However, many of the creatures were fast asleep and did not hear the warning. The bright light

from the fire startled them. The Sky Spirit contemplated
how to get around this. After much thought he decided
that someone should make a loud noise at dawn to signal
that the sun was coming. It should be loud enough that
even those asleep would hear it. But he could not decide
the best person for this job.

On one fine evening the Sky God and spirits heard the
laughter of Goo-goor-gaga the laughing donkey. They
decided that he would be the best animal for the job. They
approached him and asked him if he could laugh loudly
every day as the morning star faded and the day dawned.
They explained to Goo-goor-gaga that if he did not agree
to this there would be no bright light for the world. He felt
honored to help the world in this way and agreed to
perform this duty. Because of Goo-goor-gaga the world
was able to enjoy the beauty and brightness of the light.
Now the light worked in an interesting way.

When the spirits first lit the fire it did not give off much
heat, but by the middle of the day the heap of firewood
would give off a fierce heat and after that would fade
away into sunset where only its red embers would be left.
When those embers died out they were covered up with
the clouds by the spirits who would save them to light the
heap of wood they would get ready for the next day.

Traditional Aboriginal story adapted by **Omi**

~ 269 ~

A Warmer Planet

Global warming - a gradual increase in planet-wide temperatures -- is now well documented and accepted by scientists as fact. A panel convened by the U.S National Research Council, the nation's premier science policy body, in June 2006 voiced a "high level of confidence" that Earth is the hottest it has been in at least 400 years, and possibly even the last 2,000 years. This warming is largely attributed to the increase of greenhouse gases (primarily carbon dioxide and methane) in the Earth's upper atmosphere caused by human burning of fossil fuels, industrial, farming, and deforestation activities. Some uncertainty remains about the role of natural variations in causing climate change. Solar variability certainly plays a minor role, but it looks like only a quarter of the recent variations can be attributed to the Sun. How hot is the sun getting? The sun is getting hotter its solar radiation reaching the Earth is 0.036 percent warmer than it was in 1986. Dr Richard C. Wilson of Colombia University's center for Climate Systems Research revealed the increase is only a small fraction of the Sun's total heat, but over a century, it would be enough to seriously aggravate problems of global warming. He further revealed that most researchers expected greenhouse gases to warm the planet by 3.6 degrees Fahrenheit over the next 100 years.

Support a Cooler Planet

Do something about the warming of the planet. Support initiatives such as Al Gore's The Climate Project at www.climatecrisis.net.

Celebrate

October 2nd

World Walk to Work Day

Our Special Star

Auroras, rainbows, sun dogs, green flashes, sun pillars, sunfish, sunflowers, glorious sunrises -- the Earth is full of wondrous references to the Sun, each inspired by the life-giving force from our special star.

Stanford Solar Center

Affirmation

All is well.

The Cries of our children

Dear Father Sun,

Do you remember when he cried,

all of six years old.

"Mummy, what are we going to do?

We are all going to die.

I won't have a future anymore."

I said, "Everything is going to be okay".

He said, "no mummy that is not true, the

world is getting hotter and hotter."

Do you remember he cried for hours.

Then he said, "mummy why don't we treat the

planet better. I want to have a future. I have dreams
mummy I want to fulfill."

"and you will," I said hugging him, while looking out afar.

Omi

The Power of the Sun

To the best of our knowledge, our Sun is the only star proven to grow vegetables.

Philip Scherre

Sun Facts

Did you know?

There is a fish called the Sunfish. It is one of the strangest inhabitants of the water world. It is named for its habit of laying on its back near the surface of the water to "sunbath". This fish is known as a gentle giant with strange features. It is square, missing a tail and its fins are in the wrong place.

The sun flower tracks the sun throughout the day.

The Sun Scorpion in fact does not like the sunlight but prefers to hunt by the dark. It is also called the wind scorpion because they appear to move as fast as the wind.

Stanford Solar Center

Wings of Time

Time takes me on its wing and I travel to the sun
and am consumed by fire.
Time takes me on its wing and I travel to the river
and am drowned in water.
Time takes me on its wing and I travel into the Earth
and am a mountain not yet risen.
Each place I go others have gone before me.
That is why
the sun dances
the wind weeps
the river leaps
and the Earth sings.
Neither the sun nor the wind, the river nor the Earth
did these things
before man was placed in this world to believe it.

Taos Pueblo sayings

Celebrate

October 4th

World Animal Day

MISSION STATEMENT - WORLD ANIMAL DAY

To celebrate animal life in all its forms

To celebrate humankind's relationship with the animal kingdom

To acknowledge the diverse roles that animals play in our lives – from being our companions, supporting and helping us, to bringing a sense of wonder into our lives

To acknowledge and be thankful for the way in which animals enrich our lives.

Surya, the God of Radiance and Life

Surya Dev is perhaps the most ancient god revered in Hindu the belief system. Souram is the sect devoted to Lord Surya. Lord Surya is said to be the only god in Hindu belief who can be seen and prayed to in daily life. Why? Because Surya Dev is personified by the sun.

He is believed to be the King of all the planets and is responsible for controlling all their movements. Thus he is the major god amongst the Navgrahas of India. Surya Dev is spectacular to look at. He is a golden red man with three eyes and four arms, riding a chariot driven by seven white horses. He is the life giver and sustainer of all life on Earth. He mounts the wheel of time and is also the one who is responsible for the beautiful seasons and the cycle of day & night. In the Vedic ancient text he is referred to as the god of light who is responsible for all life on Earth.

Omi

Shadows Fall

Turn your face to the sun and the shadows fall behind
you."

Maori proverb

Amaterasu the Sun Goddess

Once upon a time there was a beautiful Goddess, so beautiful men dared not to look at her for fear of being blinded by her beauty. The beautiful Goddess was called Amaterasu. Despite her beauty and gentle personality her brother Susanowo loved teasing her and treating her badly. One day he teased her so bad that she cried and decided she would run away from him.

She waited till night fall and found a cave to hide in. The only problem was that the cave entrance was covered by a gigantic stone. She used all her strength to move the stone to one side. She went quickly into the cave and used all her strength again to roll the enormous stone to close the cave's entrance. As soon as this act was done the whole world became dark and the evil spirits were happy that Amaterasu was not around. They began to wreak havoc on Earth.

No one knew what to do about these evil spirits who did not care about anyone or anything. Then one day the Gods decided to call a conference. They came to a unanimous decision – they would trick Amaterasu into coming out of hiding by having a party near the cave. They put a big mirror in front of the cave and beautiful jewels on a tree.

Uzume, the goddess of laughter, began a dance accompanied by loud music.

Hearing the music and laughter, Amaterasu was so curious that she took a look outside to find out what was going on. She was so fascinated by her own brilliant reflection in the mirror that she came out of the cave. Finally, the beauty and force of her light covered and colored the world the world once again.

Japanese Shinto Story of the Sun and Creation adapted by

Omi

Purpose of Life

The purpose of life is the investigation of the Sun, the Moon, and the Heavens."

Anaxagoras 459 BC

Bowing to the Sun

When I close my eyes and open my mind,

I see you.

I can see you watching the horizon.

You watch how the early morning sun rises

you are enraptured by its slow seductive movements.

You bow "greetings mighty Heru".

It continues to rise in mightiness and strength.

Your hands rise in prayer "greetings Ra".

As it tires and gets ready to leave

You lower your eyes,

in reverence of its final resting place.

Omi

Solar Panels

Help the environment by considering solar panels for your house.

Pharaohs and the Sun

Our ancestors understood the importance of the sun.
Without the sun we have no life. The ancient Egyptians
saw the early morning sun as the manifestation of the God
Horus/Heru. The mid day sun was Ra and the setting sun
was the Creator himself coming to lift the spirits of the
Pharaohs to their final celestial resting place. The redness
of the setting sun was viewed as the blood from the Sun
God as he died and became associated with death and rebirth. Night became associated with death (the fading
away of the old) and day with rebirth.

Omi

The Healing Power Sweating

Rituals and the tradition of the Native American sweat lodges vary from region to region and tribe to tribe. Using intense heat to produce Sweating is part of the medical and spiritual belief system of ancient India and other cultures. It is seen as a way of releasing the body and spirit from impurities. The "sweat experience" includes prayers, drumming, and offerings to the spirit world. A sweat lodge can be a part of, or a beginning component of another, longer ceremony such as a Sun Dance.

In the sweat lodge an offering of tobacco, sweet grass, red cedar or white cedar, and other plants are made. There are also gratitude prayers and the prayers asking for healing for one self, family and others. There are those assigned to be outside the sweat to assist with the fire and to protect the ceremony.

Many report that during and after a sweat they feel purified and uplifted.

Why not try a contemporary sweat by going to a sauna or having a bath to steam your worries and stress away.

Omi - based on conversation with Danny Garris, Catawba Indian

~ 288 ~

Affirmation

Everything in the world is good today

Sun Healing Meditation

Find a quiet place, put on music that sets a warm soothing
atmosphere.

Close your eyes,

inhale,

exhale.

On your inhalation allow yourself to relax.

On your exhalation breathe out stress, worry and pain.

As you sink into a deeper state of relaxation,

imagine you are lying in the sun on

the grass.

You are by a lake.

Breathe in the warm energy of the sun.

Allow its warmth to travel to each part of your body.

You relax more and more.

Allow yourself to enjoy this state.

When you are ready slowly open your eyes.

Omi

Sun Meditation for Emotional Healing

The energy center within the body that governs how you feel about your inner self, power and identity

is known as the solar chakra. Located in the top center of your abdomen it is associated with the power of the sun. When balanced it makes you feel confident and good . about yourself. In a bodily sense this energy center governs immunity, digestion, liver and the nervous system.

Those who are domineering or shy have an imbalanced solar center.

To re-balance your solar chakra, find a quiet space. Against a backdrop of gentle music inhale and exhale until you feel yourself enter a state of deep relaxation.

Once relaxed breathe in the colour yellow. Imagine it gently traveling to every part of your body and healing it. The energy especially focuses on the abdomen.

Repeat this exercise whenever you feel a drop in your self-esteem and focus.

Omi

~ 291 ~

Sun Meditation for Our Children

Find a quiet place,

put on some calming music.

Close your eyes.

Inhale and breathe in the warmth of relaxation.

Exhale and breathe out all the negative emotions and
tension.

As you sink into a deeper state of relaxation

imagine you are lying in the sun on

beautiful green grass,

in a magical forest.

Allow the warm golden energy of the sun,

travels to each part of your body making you feel so
relaxed.

Enjoy.

Omi

Sun Salutation Greeting

Sun Salutation is a series of yoga poses performed in a graceful flow and linked by breath—a method called vinyasa. It's a great way to greet the sun any time of the day. It originated as a sunrise greeting to the Hindu God Surya.

You will need comfortable clothing suitable for stretching and moving,

a calm place where you won't be distracted or disturbed and a yoga mat or folded blanket.

Step 1: Mountain Pose

Stand at the front of your mat in the Mountain Pose, with your feet hip-width apart and your weight evenly distributed between them, your spine erect, and your arms at your sides.

Step 2: Arms Reaching Upward

Inhale into the Arms Reaching Upward Pose, extending your arms overhead, bringing your palms together, and expanding your chest.

Step 3: Standing Forward Bend

Exhale into the Standing Forward Bend, bringing your chest toward your thighs and your hands toward the floor.

Step 4: Lung Pose

Inhale into the Lunge Pose, placing your hands on the mat on either side of your right foot as you lunge your left leg straight back behind you. Expand your chest as you lengthen your spine.

Step 5: Plank Pose

Exhale into the Plank Pose, stepping your right leg back so your feet are now side by side. Look straight at the floor, keeping your arms extended and your body straight. Hold this pose for 3 to 5 full breaths.

Step 6: Kneel & lower head

Exhale, slowly dropping your knees to the floor. Untuck your toes, bring your hips back to your heels, and lower your head to the floor with your arms still extended in front of you.

Step 7: Get on all fours

Inhale, slowly bringing yourself up on all fours.

Step 8: Lower chest & chin

Exhale, slowly bending your elbows and lowering your chest and chin to the floor so your hands, knees, and feet are touching the mat.

Step 9: Upward Facing Dog

Inhale into the Upward Facing Dog Pose, pushing your head and ribcage up off the mat by fully extending your arms as you press the tops of your feet into the ground. Your thighs and hips should rise a few inches above the mat.

Step 10: Downward Facing Dog

Exhale into the Downward Facing Dog Pose, tucking your toes and lifting your hips up and back so that you're bearing your weight on the balls of your feet. This should create an upside-down V shape with your body. Relax your neck and allow the weight of your head to lengthen your spine.

Step 11: Lung Pose

Inhale into the Lunge Pose again, stepping your left foot forward.

Step 12: Standing Forward Bend

Exhale into the Standing Forward Bend again, stepping your right foot forward next to your left foot so your weight is on both feet.

Step 13: Arms Reaching Upward

Inhale into the Arms Reaching Upward Pose again.

Step 14: Mountain Pose

Exhale, completing the Sun Salutation by returning to the Mountain Pose.

Omi

Who has doing the Sun Salutation for over fifteen years.

Morning Fire Up

The element of the sun is represented in nature and our bodies. In the ancient Indian text of Ayurveda (Ayu=Science, Veda = knowledge of life) it is stated that many illness

are caused when our digestive fire and metabolic power is weak. Low digestive power is caused by

bad eating habits which result in toxins which in turn result in disease.

A way to ensure the digestive power remains fired up is to cut out refined carbohydrates, junk food, caffeine, fizzy drinks and over eating, late night eating. Also, drink this simple but powerful concoction that will help you to feel more

energized, less fatigued and it even burns cellulite. So what is this magic bullet? Simply mix a few sprinkles of cayenne pepper, black pepper, honey and ginger in warm water and drink before your morning meal. –This ancient fat burning metabolic boosting drink is known as Trikatu.

Omi

~ 297 ~

Sunrise

Try and catch the sunrise.

Celebrate

October 5th

World Habitat Day

The United Nations has designated the first Monday in October every year as World Habitat Day to reflect on the state of human settlements and the basic right to adequate shelter for all. It is also intended to remind the world of its collective responsibility for the future of the human habitat.

~ 299 ~

Affirmation

I embrace all good things in life.

Sunset

Watch a beautiful sunset.

Earth Reflection Notes

Earth Reflection Notes

Earth Reflection Notes

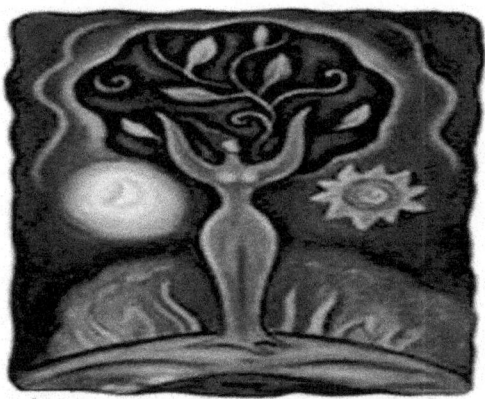

Space and Air

Space and Air

Somewhere and somehow, as I journeyed with water, I became aware of the sacred element of space and air It might have been somewhere between contemplating the magnetic essence of water, watching its meandering over obstacles or marveling at its infinite sparkles when the presence of space and air inched in to fill my awareness.

Space is the sacred element that fills our sphere of awareness quietly and without fanfare. It enters the pores of our daily activities unseen and unheard. Deep in its essence lies the mystery of the beginning of life that began with the Big Bang and the hurtling of life dust to all corners of its universe. Captivating the world in its universal chant of OM which flung open the eyes of all of life. As it breathlessly awoke life the Hindu ancients say that the element of air was born. To it all movement is assigned.

For it is air we first gulp in as we ease out from our mother's womb with fist raised in victory, and marvel in our eyes. We gasp as the life of air, Prana, Chi, Vital Life Force and the life giving gas of oxygen rush through our blood. This ritual is repeated in species across globes and worlds.

78% nitrogen and 21% oxygen make up the matrix that we call air. Those who stared into the nights skies who wondered about the mysteries of life said it contained the breath of the creator itself. No wonder they believed this for it provides the gases that plants need for survival and the oxygen animals need for living.

Air is delicate. So delicate that small shifts can affect it drastically. Characterized by the beautiful, transformation energy of the West African Goddess Oya and Hindu God Vayu, air can mesmerize us with showers, mist, storms, floods and droughts. It is always moving, always restless as it does the stomp dance rising by day to the glory of the sun's warmth and falling by night as the sun begins to tuck away for sleep.

Gratitude to the Universe

Dear Universal consciousness,
How can I forget you?
I cannot.
You gave me wisdom,
feelings,
emotions,
sight,
movement,
creativity,
life,
health,
wealth,
children,
companionship,
faith,
love,
compassion,
Spirit,
a beautiful world to live in and look after
Thank you.

Omi

From Consciousness We All Come

All things came from universal consciousness which
created the fundamental elements of life known as
panchamahabhutas. They are space, air, wind, fire and
earth. They in turn became the building blocks for
everything we see in our material world. Therefore, the
universal consciousness is in everything we behold,
including ourselves.

*Omi sharing the views on the creation of the world from the
ancient Indian Vedic text*

Dark Matter

Remarkably, it turns out there is five times more material
in clusters of galaxies than we would expect from the
galaxies and hot gases we can see. Most of the stuff in
clusters of galaxies is invisible, and since these are the
largest structures in the Universe, held together by gravity,
scientists then conclude that most of the matter in the
entire Universe is invisible. This invisible stuff is called
dark matter.

Nasa

In Honor of David Bohm

David Bohm was born in Wilkes-Barre, Pennsylvania in 1917. He died on 27 October 1992. He became interested in science from an early age and went on to become one of the most distinguished theoretical physicists of his time. He was described by many as selfless and sharing. In the words of one of his former students, "He can only be characterized as a secular saint."

His interests and influence extended far beyond physics and embraced biology, psychology, philosophy, religion art and the future of society. He stated the belief by individuals that they are separate from each other and all things, was a fundamental problem that underline society's problem. For Bohm there lay a deeper underlying order of undivided wholeness which he called "quantum potential." He said that it could also be called "idealism, spirit, consciousness."

Bohm challenged the view of orthodox quantum physics that subatomic particles had no existence besides what you behold through the eye and did things by chance. For Bohm matter was a product of universal energy and the two were therefore one. He further believed that the underlying energy of all things existed in everything, which folded and unfolded it creating all

~ 311 ~

matter including supposedly "inanimate" matter such as electrons or plasmas. All matter had a "proto intelligence" therefore evolution and development of all things in life does not develop in a random fashion but as creative interrelated parts of a whole.

In 1951 Bohm published an excellent classic text called Quantum Theory in which he presented a clear account of orthodox quantum physics. However, this was at a stage where he had already begun to question the premise of this field and its assumptions. Bohm discussed his ideas with Einstein in a series of conversations which took place over six months. Einstein revealed that he too was dissatisfied with the assumptions of quantum physics. In 1952 and after their numerous discussions Bohm published two papers which he stated, ""opens the door for the creative operation of underlying, and yet subtler, levels of reality."

In 1959 Bohm and a young research student Yakir Aharonov proved that all things consisted of quantum potential (universal energy) which provided direct connections between all life systems. They discovered that in certain circumstances electrons are able to "feel" the presence of a nearby magnetic field even though they are traveling in regions of space where the field strength is zero. This phenomenon is now known as the Aharonov-

Bohm (AB) effect, and when the discovery was first announced many physicists reacted with disbelief.

In 1982 a remarkable experiment to test quantum interconnectedness was performed by a research team led by physicist Alain Aspect in Paris. The original idea was contained in a thought experiment (also known as the "EPR paradox") proposed in 1935 by Albert Einstein, Boris Podolsky, and Nathan Rosen, but much of the later theoretical groundwork was laid by David Bohm and one of his enthusiastic supporters, John Bell of CERN, the physics research center near Geneva. The results of the experiment clearly showed that subatomic particles that are far apart are able to communicate in ways that cannot be explained by the transfer of physical signals traveling faster or slower than them.

Bohm viewed all things as "subtotals" of a deeper universal energy and an unbroken wholeness. In Wholeness and Implicate Order he gives the analogy of a flowing stream.

"On this stream, one may see an ever-changing pattern of vortices, ripples, waves, splashes, etc., which evidently have no independent existence as such. Rather, they are abstracted from the flowing movement, arising and vanishing in the total process of the flow. Such transitory subsistence as may be possessed by these abstracted forms implies only a relative independence or autonomy of behavior, rather than absolutely independent existence as ultimate substances."

Another metaphor Bohm uses to illustrate the implicate order is that of the hologram. To make a hologram a laser light is split into two beams, one of which is reflected off an object onto a photographic plate where it interferes with the second beam. The complex swirls of the interference pattern recorded on the photographic plate appear meaningless and disordered to the naked eye. But the pattern possesses a hidden or enfolded order, for when illuminated with laser light it produces a three-dimensional image of the original object, which can be viewed from any angle. A remarkable feature of a hologram is that if a holographic film is cut into pieces, each piece produces an image of the whole object, though the smaller the piece the hazier the image. Clearly the form and structure of the entire object are encoded within each region of the photographic record.

Bohm's view is very much in line with the scientific view of the ancients whose creation stories show that life unfolds in stages from an intelligent universal energy which is present within all living things.

Omi, after reading about David Bohm became very impressed by his works. She gathered her knowledge from many sources including Wikipedia, Quantum Theory," New York, 1951 "Causality and Change in Modern Physics," London, 1957 "The Special Theory of Relativity," New York 1966, "Wholeness and the Implicate Order," London, 1980 "Unfolding Meaning," (record of a dialogue with David Bohm), London, 1985 , "Science, Order and Creativity," New York, 1987 , Quantum Theory," New York, 1951

Celebrate

October 16th

World Food Day

The Food and Agriculture Organization of the United
Nations celebrates World Food Day each year on 16
October, the day on which the Organization was founded
in 1945. The World Food Day and TeleFood theme for 2007
is "The Right to Food".

The Cloth of Life

We did not weave the web of life; we are merely a strand in it. Whatever we do to the web, we do to ourselves."

Chief Seattle Chief of the Duwamish, Suquamish and allied Indian tribes (~1786 - 1866)

A Big Wide World

We are part of a much larger universe than we think. The
Hubble Space Telescope (HST) site estimates there are
hundreds of billions of galaxies in the universe. A recent
German super-computer simulation estimates that the
number may be as high. The Milky Way, sometimes called
simply the Galaxy, is the galaxy in which the Solar System
is located. It is a barred spiral galaxy that is part of the
Local Group of galaxies. It is one of billions of galaxies in
the observable universe and contains billions of stars. Our
sun is just one of them.

Omi

Obatala's Ladder

The ancient Yoruba story of Obatala's ladder shows how all things are created from consciousness. Olodumare, is Yoruba for God. Obatala encapsulates God consciousness on Earth. In the story take note of his ladder. This ladder symbolizes the DNA of life. Every aspect of the story represents the fundamental elements that create life. Obatala he begins his journey in Heaven which represents: ether/space. He then gets the God of iron, Ogun, to make him a chain ladder which he climbs down through the air representing the element of air. The Earth that he puts on water represents the element of earth and water. The formation of the palm tree and humans shows how these elements came together to form different life forms. This story fits into the concept of the origins of life that is growing in the field of quantum science.

Enjoy:

One day Olodumare called Obatala to the realm of the ancestors (Ikole Orun). He wanted him to create dry land on the waters of the Earth (Ikole Aye). However Obatala stated he did not know the mystery for doing so. In response to this Olodumare (God) informed Obatala he would give him the power to make land on Earth. He gave him a snail shell filled with earth, palm nuts and a Guinea Hen On receiving these items Obatala wanted to know how he was going to make his way from the ancestral realm to Earth. Ogun, the deity of iron, stated he would create a chain to help him achieve his journey down.

On making the chain Ogun flung it down to Earth and the chain attached the realm of Heaven and Earth. Thankful, Obatala began his journey down to Earth. When he reached the last rung of the chain he noticed that he was far from the primal waters.

At that point he removed the snail shell from his pouch and sprinkled some soil upon the Primal Waters. He then removed the Guinea Hen and dropped it on the land. The hen began to scratch the land and spread the dirt across the primal waters.

Once Obatala noticed the ground had become firm he removed a palm nut and dropped it on the land. It grew to its full height and reached the last

rung of the chain. Once it did this Obatala stepped from the chain to the palm tree. Upon climbing down from the tree Obatala started to mold humans from the clay in the Earth. As he worked he became tired and decided to rest. He took fruit from the palm tree and made wine and drank until he was ready to return. The human he molded while

drunk did not resemble the others, but he did not notice.
He kept on drinking till he fell asleep.

On awakening Olodumare banned Obatala from drinking
again. When he saw what happened to the humans he had
created while drunk he agreed to protect all children for
future generations.

Om

Spirit Walk

Once upon a time there was nothingness. That all changed with a loud yawn. The spirits from beneath the Earth awoke from their eternal slumber and moved away the dirt of the earth so that they could reach its surface. They climbed onto the Earth's surface and out with them came the sun. The Earth was flooded with a brilliant light. The spirits were many different shapes. Some were shaped liked animals resembling kangaroos, emus and others emerged as women and men.

There was something very magical about these spirits. It became obvious that there was no separateness between the human, animal and plant spirit. For the spirits that were shaped as humans could change at will into animals and those that looked like animals acted like humans. These spirits were so huge that their movements on the Earth created dents, troughs, hills, mountains, rivers, plains, sand hills. All their actions, words and laws laid down formed the basis of universal law today. Every natural feature created from their movements became landmarks associated with their deeds.

The spirits composed songs about their deeds. These became the basis of their offspring's myths, stories and ceremonies. Today their children known as the Aborigines sing these songs in ceremonies and dances as they re-enact the wonderful things their ancestors created on Earth.

As the spirits continued to roam the Earth they became exhausted, and decided it was time to go back to sleep. Before they went back into the ground at the spots where they originally came from they did their last act - the sun, moon and rest of the Earth gave birth to celestial beings and rose into the sky, leaving man to wander the Earth.

Aboriginal creation story re-told by Omi

Stargazing

Go out on a fine moonlit night and watch the stars.

Celebrate

October 17th

International Day for the Eradication

Affirmation

I am whole.

Moksha

It is the fruit of our actions on Earth that determine
Moksha, personal salvation. That is what every soul
should aim for.

Concept of good actions on Earth from ancient Indian Vedic text

We Know the Stars

Starlore was passed down from generation to generation through the teachings and storytelling of the Elders. The positions of the planets and stars were used by the Aboriginals for gathering food; for finding their way from one place to another; and for the timing of rituals and ceremonies.

Om

Egyptian Star Gazers

When the Greek historian Herodotus visited Egypt in
about 450 BC, he noted that Egyptian astrologers "can tell
what fortune and what end and what disposition a man
shall have according to the day of his birth…

When an ominous thing happens they take note of the
outcome and write it down, and if something of a like kind
happens again, they think it will have a like result?"

From this account it is clear that the Egyptians were
engaging in a rational and carefully researched
examination of the relationship between the planets and
events on Earth.

Julia & Derek Parker, Astrology

Celebrate

November 21

World Fisheries Day

World Fisheries day is celebrated every year on November 21 throughout the world by the fisher folk communities. Fishing communities worldwide celebrate this day through rallies, workshops, public meetings, cultural programs, dramas, exhibitions, music shows, and demonstrations to highlight the importance of maintaining the world's fisheries.

A recent United Nations study reported that more than two-thirds of the world's fisheries have been over fished or are fully harvested and more than one third are in a state of decline because of factors such as the loss of essential fish habitats, pollution, and global warming.

The World Fisheries Day helps in highlighting the critical importance of water to human lives.

Omi

~ 330 ~

The Sirius Star System and the Dogons

In the 1930's two French anthropologists, Marcel Griaule and Germain Dieterlen recorded secret knowledge of the Dogons from Mali, West Africa. Many say the Dogons originally came from ancient Egypt. The information about Dogon culture and belief systems was obtained from four Dogon priests.

According to their oral traditions, a race of people from the Sirius system called the Nommos visited Earth thousands of years ago. The Nommos were ugly, amphibious beings that resembled mermen and mermaids. These beings also appear in Babylonian, Accadian, and Sumerian myths. The Egyptian Goddess Isis, who is sometimes depicted as a mermaid, is also linked with the star Sirius.

The Dogons have a four hundred year old artifact that depicts the Sirius configuration and the Sigui ceremony they have held since the 13th century to celebrate the cycle of Sirius A. The ceremony takes place every 65 years and can take several years to complete. The last one started in 1967 and ended in 1973, the next one will begin in 2032. The Sigui ceremony is fascinating. It symbolizes the very first ancestors who roamed the Earth and till the moment that humanity acquired the use of the spoken word. The ceremony is a long procession that starts and ends in the Dogon village of Youga Dogorou. It goes from one village to the other during several months or years. All men wear masks and dance in long processions. The ceremony has a secret language that women are not allowed to learn.

The secret Society of Sigui plays a central role in the ceremony. They prepare the ceremonies a long time in advance, and they live for three months hidden outside of the villages out of human sight. The men from the Society of Sigui are called the Oloubarou. The villagers are afraid of them. This fear is reinforced by a prohibition to go out at night, when sounds warn that the Oloubarou are out. The most important mask that plays a major role in the Sigui rituals is the Great Mask or the Mother of Masks. It is several meters long and is held up by hand above the head. This mask is newly created every 65 years.

Omi

A Small Discourse

Creation in most ancient cultures is represented by complex cosmological systems that explain the origins and principles of maintenance for the world. They all believed in one Supreme Being that manifested itself in many dynamic forms. The Supreme Being was the infinite universal essence from whence all things come and return. In the ancient Indian tradition God is seen as represented by three dynamic principles Lord Brahma the Creator, Lord Vishnu the Preserver, and Lord Shiva the Destroyer. Each one is depicted with a Goddess as his companion who is said to represent the dynamic creative power and energy of creation itself. The same is true with the Yoruba of West Africa who have Olodumare known to be the ultimate creator. He has elements such as Obatala, Orunmila, Osun and Esu as his dynamic life forces. Obatala represents consciousness itself, Orunmila represents the wisdom faculty of God, Esu represents the gate keeper of God's universal order, while the Goddess represents the holder of life itself. We can mention many more cultures, but we will see the same truth repeated over and over again.

Omi

~ 333 ~

The Festival of Shiva

Mahashivaratri (also called Shiva Ratri) is the great festival of Shiva, the God of Re-creation. This exciting festival is held during the month of March. Mahashivaratri is especially important to Saivites (devotees of Shiva), but it is celebrated by most Hindus.

The day of Mahashivaratri is spent in meditation on Shiva and fasting (some may take water or fruit). Temples dedicated to Shiva are filled with many devotees offering prayers. The Shiva statue at the temple or in one's home is bathed with milk, honey and water, and offerings are made to Shiva in the form of Bilva leaves, fruits, and other specially prepared foods. Offering Bilva leaves to Shiva on Mahashivaratri is considered especially auspicious.

Devotees sing hymns and chant mantras, especially Om Namah Shivaya.

Some sit around a sacred fire and toss offerings of grain into the flames while chanting to Shiva. After fasting and meditating throughout the day, a vigil is held all night with continued prayers and meditation.

Various legends are associated with the holiday of Mahashivaratri. One is the popular legend of the Churning of the Ocean of Milk, in which the gods inadvertently unearthed a poison that threatened to destroy the world. Shiva saved the day by drinking the poison, which accounts for his blue throat in some Hindu art.

It is said that Shiva was strong enough to handle the poison, but he had to stay awake all night as part of his healing. The other gods helped get him through the night by entertaining him with dances and other distractions. This is commemorated on Mahashivaratri, when Shiva's followers keep him company through the night.

Another legend tells the story of a hunter who climbed a Bilva tree to escape a hungry lion. The lion sat down beneath the tree and waited for the hunter to fall. As he waited in the tree all night, the hunter plucked leaves from the Bilva tree to stay awake. The leaves, which are sacred to Shiva, fell on a Shiva linga that happened to be at the base of the tree. Shiva was pleased by the offering, inadvertent though it was, and saved the hunter. This event is commemorated on Mahashivaratri by staying up all night and offering Bilva leaves.

Omi - adapted from stories of the Festival of Shiva

Meditation for Awakening Intuition

The brow chakra is located between the eye brows. It relates to the element of space and universal consciousness. It is connected to the pituitary, thalamus and hypothalamus glands. It is the site of the "third eye", which gives us our insight, intuition and inspiration. This chakra gives us our power of imagination. Problems with it lead to sinus problems, stagnation in thinking and intuition. To balance and awaken your brow chakra do the following:

1. Find a quiet space
2. Play some peaceful music
3. Sit or lie in a comfortable position
4. Inhale and exhale allowing each breath to relax you
5. To help aid your relaxation, breathe in relaxation on your in-breath, breathe out stress on your out breath
6. As you sink deeper and deeper into relaxation begin to breathe in the color blue. Allow this beautiful peaceful color to flow through and relax your entire body.
7. Slowly open your eyes when you feel ready to awaken from your meditation

Half an hour to forty minutes is a good time to allocate for this exercise.

Enjoy!

Omi

~ 336 ~

Meditation for Inner Connection

The crown chakra is located on the top of the head .It is associated with the element of ether and the universal energy of consciousness. It is also connected to the pituitary gland found at the base of the brain. The pituitary gland is responsible for releasing particular hormones and is referred to as the master gland as it affects so many other glands and bodily functions. The crown chakra governs co-ordination at every level including poor balance, learning difficulties, dyslexia and the ability for us to live an overall balanced life.

1. Find a quiet space
2. Play some peaceful music
3. Sit or lie in a comfortable position
4. Inhale and exhale allowing each slow breath to relax you
5. To help aid your relaxation, breathe in relaxation on your in-breath, breathe out stress on your out breath
6. As you sink deeper and deeper into relaxation begin to breathe in the color purple. Allow this beautiful peaceful color to flow through and relax your entire body.

To enhance your meditation hold an amethyst crystal known for creating complete balance.
When you feel ready slowly open your eyes.

Omi

Inner Connection Meditation for Our Children

You are in a beautiful forest,
lying on warm grass.
You feel the warm sun on your body.
You breathe in this warmth,
the more you breathe it in is the more relaxed you feel.
You sink deeper and deeper into a state of relaxation.
As the warmth flows and fills your body up
you can feel yourself smiling, feeling more peaceful,
loving, and happy.
You feel at total one with yourself.
Enjoy this feeling,
stay with it for as long as possible.
When it is time you will awaken from this beautiful
state of relaxation.
Stretch and know this feeling can always and
will always be with you.
Any time you are afraid or angry just remember the
warmth of the sun on your face and all the good feelings
you felt.
Give yourself a big hug, and affirm
"I am loveable".

Omi

~ 338 ~

Affirmation

Today I embrace a loving world.

Celebrate

December 5th

International Volunteer Day

International Volunteer Day (IVD) was established by the United Nations General Assembly in 1985. IVD is now celebrated worldwide with thousands of volunteers involved in a range of IVD initiatives including clean-up campaigns, conferences, exhibitions, morning teas and many other activities all aimed to highlight the role of volunteers in their communities.

.

Dear Mother Wind

Thank you for your cool touch
that transforms my tired mind.
And your tireless whispers
that helps me to know who I am
Thank you for reminding me to
look up at the blue skies,
and wish on a white cloud.
For blowing the seeds,
so that they can nourish the world.
Thank you for being the drum,
that alerts me to what is to come.
For being
the effortless knowledge that
awakens my consciousness.
The timelessness of my knowing.
Thank you Mother Wind
Thank you.

Om

The Air Factor

The ancients acknowledged the element of air as one of the
fundamental elements that creates life.

It's the dynamic principle that represents movement,

and transformation.

It is represented within every aspect of our environment,

both internal and external.

Air is the element that helps things like water to move

within the plant and the roots of a tree,

it helps the transportation and contraction of things.

It is connected to creativity,

intelligence and bright ideas.

When your head is clouded,

What do you say?

"I need some air."

Omi

The Air is Precious

The air is precious to the red man for all things share the
same breath, the beast, the tree, the man; they all share the
same breath.

Chief Seattle, chief of the Suquamis

All

The cosmos is all there is, all there ever was, and all there ever will be

Carl Sagan

Upon The Shoulders of our Ancestors

The wind and air traditionally represent the power of ancestors to sustain and transform the world.

Honor the wind and our atmosphere by

offering a special prayer of thanks to the ancestors.

The wind reminds us that upon the shoulders of the

Ancestors we stand.

Honor the wind and our atmosphere by

cutting down on carbon emissions

and your carbon footprint.

Honor the wind and our atmosphere

by saving and protecting our trees.

Omi

Clean Air

Air quality is important simply because we can't avoid breathing in the air around us. The average adult breathes in about 20 cubic meters, or 20,000 liters of air a day! Those of us who live in cities should be especially concerned, since we are exposed to a greater amount of pollutants coming from automobile traffic, commercial, industrial and manufacturing facilities, as well as other sources.

Air pollutants can cause a variety of health problems -including breathing problems; asthma, reduced lung function, lung damage, bronchitis, cancer, and brain and nervous system damage. They are especially hazardous to young children.

Air pollution causes haze and smog and reduces visibility, dirties and damages buildings and other landmarks, and harms trees, lakes and animals. It is also responsible for thinning the protective ozone layer in the upper atmosphere that protects us from harmful ultraviolet radiation from the sun, and may be contributing to the phenomenon known as global warming- the steady increase in average temperature of the global climate.

Omi

www.cleanairworld.org & www.cleanairpartners.net

Mama Oya

Mama

they say you are tall and dark,

gentle,

yet strong,

fierce but kind,

beautiful but fearsome.

They say that

when I am in trouble you protect me

and when I am the trouble you reprimand me.

They say that you guard the ancestors

and the magnetic forces.

They say that without you

transformation

and renewal would be no more.

Mama I tremble to say your name,

Yet my heart grows warm with the love you show.

Omi. In honor of Oya the ancient Yoruba Goddess of wind and

transformation

The Greek Gods of the Four Winds

Aeolus - king of winds
Boreas - north wind
Zephyr - west wind
Notus - south wind
Eurus - east wind

Omi

Vayu, the Hindu God of Wind

Vayu is the Hindu god of the wind. Extremely handsome in appearance, he moves about noisily in a shiny chariot drawn by a pair of red or purple horses. He is also represented as a fair-complexioned man riding a deer and carrying a white flag. He may have two to four hands and may carry a goad and a wheel.

Often associated with Indra, the Hindu God of War and Weather Vayu won the race for the first cup of Soma juice (ambrosia). Despite his radiance he does not occupy a very prominent position in the sacred Indian hymns. He is considered to be a good friend of the waters. At a later stage he is said to have begotten a son, Hanuman (the monkey god), who played a conspicuous role in the famous and ancient epic Ramayana.

Omi

Constant of Nature

Man's law changes with his understanding of man. Only
the laws of the spirit remain always the same.

Native American quote

Cherokee Blessing

May the warm winds of Heaven blow softly on your home

and the Great Spirit bless all who enter there.

May your moccasins make happy tracks in many snows.

And may the rainbow always touch your shoulders.

A Cherokee blessing

Earth Reflection Notes

Earth Reflection Notes

_____
_____
_____
_____
_____
_____
_____
_____
_____
_____
_____
_____
_____
_____
_____
_____
_____
_____
_____
_____
_____
_____
_____

Earth Reflection Notes

Love and Gratitude

Love and Gratitude

August 2009, my husband and I frantically prepared for the second Humanity4Water award ceremony. We did it from our own pockets, with very little money, but we were determined to honor those who like ourselves who had decided to take the responsibility of being good planetary Stewards again. Sometimes, I wondered if we were crazy for doing a ceremony which was putting so much strain on us. But we were driven by the tremendous love we had for the rivers, all the sacred elements of life, our children, and humanity. We were also deeply moved by the love of those we were honoring, the ones who had dared to care and do something to secure the future of all generations.

Ultimately, I think the spirit of water taught me love and gratitude. The more I contemplated its gentle flow, its sustaining nature, its endless giving - was the more I seemed to contemplate the unconditional nature of love that seemed to ooze from the green pores of all living things and the gratitude that sustains that flow.

It was in the arms of Amma; known as a Universal Mother and Hugging Saint I experienced Love vs. love. In July 2009 my husband and I made our way to Washington on a stretched dollar to give Amma her Humanity4Water award in the area of Compassion. We were fortunate to be seated right next to her light filled presence. Because of her devotion to healing through love and action she is known to hug thousands of people a day. She hugs the young, old, diseased, and well. I did not know that Love could transform so deeply until Amma enfolded me into her arms. The world went dark; it felt as though nothing else existed but the universe. In that hug my heart became fused with the unity of all things and filled with the gratitude of the immense blessing I felt.

As Amma said, "Love is our true essence. Love has no limitations of caste, religion, race or nationality. We are all beads strung together on the same thread of love"

So what really is this thing called love? In the West we see love as sexual and physical intimacy but author of "The Sacred Balance," David Suzuki suggest that love is "a sacred element." From the time we are babies to the day we die we rely on the love and compassion of others. When a baby does not receive love it shows up as dense lines on x rays of their bones. The lines indicate periods when love was lacking and growth does not occur.

I remember reading an article in the Reader's Digest April 2008 edition. "Learning to Love" was the title that blazed in orange across the page. The small summary read, "seven years in a Romanian orphanage left Daniel Solomon broken and full of rage. How his new American family healed him and themselves". It was all topped of with a picture of the handsome face of a Romanian boy and the loving smile of his adoptive mother. My appetite was whetted enough for me to turn the page to discover the story behind the picture and title.

From the ages of 0 to five Daniel had spent his life in a Romanian orphanage. It was more like "a prison than a home for parentless children. Daniel was affectionate when he was adopted but he soon showed signs of severe behavior disorder as he "smashed toys and assaulted other kids". He was also committed to a psychiatric hospital.

What was behind Daniel's behavior? The article explains, "he had never owned a pair of shoes, never been read to, never gotten a hug. He didn't even know he had parents." If Heidi Solomon and her husband knew what they would be getting themselves into I wonder if they would have still adopted Daniel. But they did. Heidi says that at first his behavior was normal (despite a few tantrums). Then one day he turned eight and had a birthday party.

Instead of being a time of celebration it marked a long road of rage and fury as Daniel realized "someone had brought him into the world and abandoned him". Unfortunately, he believed that "someone" was his adoptive father and mother. Even though they tried to explain to him they weren't his biological parents his anger needed something to fix itself on and they became the "it" from childhood games.

They tried to help him as much they could. They bought him a puppy; he tried to strangle it. They took him to therapists; he bit a three inch gash in the stomach of one. They sent him to a good school; he threatened his principal with a shard of glass. They gave him as much love as humanly possible; he head butted his mother, gave her a black eye and took a knife to her throat. Daniel not only loathed his new parents, he loathed himself. He contemplated suicide many times.

According to psychotherapist Daniel was suffering from attachment-disorder. It simply means someone who believes they are bad, unwanted, worthless and unlovable. As a result they are unable to receive or demonstrate love. While the disorder is rare it is commonly found in abused children, including the thousands adopted in the United States every year from "warehouse-style" Eastern European orphanages.

Most individuals would have abandoned Daniel out of frustration, washed their hands of him but Heidi and her husband did not. Their love kept them going, their knowledge that he needed love also kept them trying to find solutions. Institutions and drugs did not work. So

Heidi decided she would try a different approach. There was a gentler way of healing according to Ronald Federici, a Virginia neuropsychologist. Albeit gentle it was very demanding. For two months solid Heidi and her husband had to stand three feet from Daniel. He was not to ask for anything but food and clothes. He had to maintain eye contact each and every time he asked for something. The therapy was based on re-creating the mother-baby bond they had never developed. A bond Daniel had never developed with anyone.

Daniel began to change and transform. He became more loving, appreciated how much his parents had done for him. Then to everyone's amazement Daniel received his synagogue award for most outstanding high school student. He then said three words to his parents he had never said before, "I love you".

Today Daniel is still in therapy, the lack of love he received in his life means he has great trouble reading and writing. He will not be able to go to college but he now wants to give back the love he received and learned to recognize by becoming a fire man.

It is no wonder Bernie Siegal, surgeon and author commented in his book, "Peace, Love and Healing" – "the world would be a better place with love". The basis of his statement is rooted in the fact that the Pygmies of South

Africa who demonstrate a lot of touching and affection have no crime, no infidelity, no stigma against sexuality and a great respect, "not only for each other, especially the elders amongst them, but for the forest in which they dwell."

His Holiness The fourteenth Dalai Lama Tenzin Gyatso of Tibet shares, "all phenomenon from the planet we inhabit to the oceans, clouds, forests, and flowers that surround us, arise independence upon subtle patterns of energy. Without their proper interaction they dissolve and decay." He further states it is this independence which results in our need and desire for love. As Amma shares, "there are two types of poverty in the world, financial poverty and poverty of love, the second is more important." As the second creates the first.

It would seem that David Suzuki, author of "The Sacred Balance" was right when he stated love is another element. However, I would like to add that I think Gratitude is also an element that helps sustain the nourishing flow of our world. Gratitude goes hand in hand with Love. In Daniel's story his love is accompanied by large measures of gratitude. It seems to be the vessel that allows his love to be expressed and grow. As my husband said, "I sincerely believe gratitude is love unveiled."

As part of the Humanity4Water Project and Awards we are now launching The White Cloth of Compassion Project. The idea is simple - to give a White Cloth of Compassion to as many people as possible. Who will keep it as a statement of our unified commitment to fill the world with love and compassion.

After four years, to date, of doing the Humanity4Water Project and Awards we have discovered only loving and compassionate action can bring us back from the brink of what scientist are now calling the sixth extinction.

The Grace of Giving

As a child I understood how to give; I have forgotten this grace since I have become civilized.

Chief Luther Standing Bear, Oglala Siou

Working Together

Survival of the world depends on our sharing what we
have, and working together. If we don't the whole world
will die. First the planet, and next the people.

Chief Frank Fools Crow, Teton Sioux

Celebrate

December 3rd

International Day for People with Disabilities

On December 3 every year, International Day of People with Disability (IDPwD) is celebrated worldwide recognizing the achievements and contributions of people with disability

The Voice of the Great Spirit

The voice of the
Great Spirit
is heard in the
twittering of birds,
the rippling
of mighty waters
and the sweet
breathing of flowers.
If this is Paganism,
then at present,
at least,
I am a Pagan.

Zitkala-Sa (1887-1938) Dakota Sioux Quotes

Meditation for Healing the Heart

The heart chakra is in the center of the chest. It is connected to the expansive and transforming element of air. It is also located at the thymus gland. This chakra governs the heart and controls our ability to show compassion, love to others and ourselves. It has a powerful influence on our relationship with the divine and the outside world. It governs our ability to freely express ourselves. When the heart chakra is not matured or opened properly it leads to the person withholding their feelings and being stingy with her affections. It can also lead to the other extreme of seeking love in all the wrong places and over giving that leads to physical and emotional exhaustion. Tightness or pain in the chest is an indicator that the heart chakra is out of balance.

1. Find a quiet space
2. Play some peaceful music
3. Sit or lie in a comfortable position
4. Inhale and exhale slowly yourself to relax
5. As you sink deeper into relaxation breathe in the colour pink or green allowing it to fill your entire body. A rose quartz or a green coloured crystal will aid your meditation.

Omi

~ 367 ~

Meditation for Healing the Inner Voice

The throat chakra is in the base of the throat. It is related to the element air. It is also connected to the thyroid and parathyroid glands. This chakra rules our ability to communicate with others and to express our authentic self. Difficulties in this area can lead to throat problems, such as hoarseness, tightness, dryness, soreness, and a feeling that something is stuck in that area. A blocked throat chakra will affect how we communicate our inner feelings, thoughts, self, and creativity to the outside world. .

1. Find a quiet space
2. Play some peaceful music
3. Sit or lie in a comfortable position
4. Inhale and exhale slowly allowing each breath to relax you
5. As you sink deeper and deeper into relaxation breathe in the colour light blue. Allow this beautiful peaceful colour to flow through and relax your entire body.
6. A blue lace or any blue coloured crystal will aid in your meditation.
7. On completion of your meditation open your eyes slowly.

Omi

Affirmation

Today I embrace love.

Compassion

Ultimately, the reason why love and compassion bring the greatest happiness is simply that our nature cherishes them above all else. The need for love lies at the very foundation of human existence. It results from the profound interdependence we all share with one another. However capable and skillful an individual may be, left alone, he or she will not survive. However vigorous and independent one may feel during the most prosperous periods of life, when one is sick or very young or very old, one must depend on the support of others.

Inter-dependence, of course, is a fundamental law of nature. Not only higher forms of life but also many of the smallest insects are social beings who, without any religion, law or education, survive by mutual cooperation based on an innate recognition of their interconnectedness. The most subtle level of material phenomena is also governed by interdependence. All phenomena from the planet we inhabit to the oceans, clouds, forests and flowers that surround us arise in dependence upon subtle patterns of energy. Without their proper interaction, they dissolve and decay.

14th Dalai Lama, Tenzin Gyatso, Tibet

~ 370 ~

Celebrate

December 11th

International Mountain Day

It was the UN General Assembly who designated 11 December, from 2003 onwards, as 'International Mountain Day'. This decision results from the success of the UN International Year of Mountains in 2002, which increased global awareness of the importance of mountains, stimulated the establishment of national committees in 78 countries and strengthened alliances through promoting the creation of the International Partnership for Sustainable Development in Mountain Regions, known as the 'Mountain Partnership (WSSD, Johannesburg, 2 September 2002). FAO was the designated lead coordinating agency for International Year of Mountains and is mandated to lead observance of International Mountain Day.

Affirmation

Today I give something back.

Buddhism and ecology

The premise of Zen Buddhist ecology is this: When we understand what we really are, we will be at peace with ourselves and our environment. We will cease trying to enlarge ourselves through possessions and power, take responsibility for our universal self -- the world -- and start living to give, rather than get.

A life of wisdom is a life in harmony with the natural world. In an age where filthy refuse washes up on shorelines, where we raze vast forests by the minute, where we pollute the air and water with chemicals, the thought of living in harmony with the natural world seems a long-forgotten dream. Like a sand castle swept away by waves we are eroding the very foundation of our existence. Still, we can return to a simpler, more careful, watchful way of life -- if we know the path.

The foundations of ecology in Zen Buddhism

by Ven. Sunyana Graef, Religious Education, Vol. 85. Issue

Love and Compassion

Children, love can accomplish anything and everything.
Love can cure diseases. Love can heal wounded hearts and
transform human minds. Through love one can overcome
all obstacles. Love can help us renounce all physical,
mental and intellectual tensions and thereby bring peace
and happiness.

*Sri Mata Amritanandamayi Devi, also known as Amma,
meaning Mother*

Universal Responsibility

I believe that to meet the challenge of our times, human beings will have to develop a greater sense of universal responsibility. Each of us must learn to work not for his or her self, family or nation, but for the benefit of all mankind. Universal responsibility is the real key to human survival. It is the best foundation for world. Peace, the equitable use of natural resources and through concern for the future generations, the proper care of the environment.

Extract of Speech by Dalai Lama given on June 7, 1992 to the Parliamentary Earth Summit (Global Forum) of the United Nations Conference on Environment and Development (UNCED) held in Rio de Janeiro. Brazil

The Hug that Heals

"Every emotion that you can think of has a vibration," she says. "Love is a very special, very uplifting vibration. "That's what I'm trying to give people. It's like visiting a perfume factory. Consciously or unconsciously you will carry that fragrance around with you."

When asked what she gets out of hugging people, she lets out a short, excited giggle, as though the question had caught her by surprise.

"I don't expect anything from anyone. My life is to give, not to take."

By Mario Cacciottolo, BBC News, A hug from Amma.

For 30 years Indian spiritual leader Mata Amritanandamayi, also known as Amma has been hugging people to spread the message of love and compassion. She believes compassion will help us to heal the world. A lack of it is the root cause of our planet's problems

The Heart of Nature Teaches Me

Being with nature has this amazing ability to open up
our feelings of compassion.

It helps us to realize we are connected with all things,
and all things are connected with us.

We suddenly see nature as a friend,

and we begin to wonder how that friend is.

We notice when our friend is happy and when our friend
is sad.

We then want to do something good for our friend.

That is how it is to be with nature.

Omi

Hug Exercise

Give a hug to someone today

Get a White Cloth of Compassion

Let's get real and give the planet a large dose of
compassion. Get your White Cloth of Compassion from
www.yeyeosun.com.

Affirmation

Today I honor life

Earth Reflection Notes

Earth Reflection Notes

_____
_____
_____
_____
_____
_____
_____
_____
_____
_____
_____
_____
_____
_____
_____
_____
_____
_____
_____
_____
_____
_____
_____
_____

Earth Reflection Notes

Bibliography

Aiken, Bill. Seven Sacred Rivers. Penguin Books, 1992.

Barton, Robert. The Oceans. London. Aldus Books, 1980.

Batchelor, Stephen. The Tibet Guide. Wisdom Publishers, 1987.

Beal, Merrill. Chief Joseph and the Nez Perce War. University of Washington Press, 1996.

Bohm, David. 1957. Causality and Chance in Modern Physics, 1961 Harper edition reprinted in 1980 by Philadelphia: U of Pennsylvania Press

Bohm, David. Causality and Chance in Modern Physics. University of Pennsylvania Press, 1980

Bohm, David. The Special Theory of Relativity. W.A. Benjamin, 1965.

Bohm, David. Wholeness and Implicate Order. Ark paperback Routledge, 1980.

Burchac, Joseph. Moons on The Turtle Back: A Native American Year of Moons. Putman and Grossnet Group, 1977.

Butree, M Julia. The Rhythm of the Redman: In Song, Dance and Decoration. A.S Barnes, 1930.

Carson, Rachel. The Sea Around Us. Oxford University Press, 1961.

Chief Joseph. That All People May Be One People, Send Rain to Wash The Face of The Earth. Mountain Meadow Press, 1995.

Cleary, Thomas and Sartaz, Aziz. Twilight Goddess: Spritual Feminism and Feminine Spirituality. Shambala, 2002.

Coleman, Daniel, Ecological Intelligence. Broadway Books, 2009.

Demott, Barbara. Dogon Mask. UMI Research Press, 1971.

Eckart, Edona. Bengal Tiger. Children's Press, 2003.

Eckart, Edona. Bengal Tiger. Children's Press, 2003.

Fitzgerald, Michael. Yellowtail, Crow Medicine Man and Sun Dance Chief. University of Olkahoma Press, 1991.

Fitzgerald, Michael. Yellowtail, Crow Medicine Man and Sun Dance Chief. University of Olkahoma Press, 1991.

Ghanaian Festivals:www.gsu.edu/afinijws/emmal/html

Gibbons, Boyd. "Do We Treat Our Soil Like Dirt?". National Geographic, 1984, pp 350-390.

Gore, Al. Earth in Balance: Ecology & The Human Spirit. Houghton Mifflin, 1992

Gray, Martin. Sacred Earth. Sterling Publishing, 2007.

Gribbin John. Our Changing Planet.Thomas Y. Crowell Co., 1977.

H. Ronald, Bailey. Gacier. Time-Life Books, 1982.

Hawkins, Stephen. The Universe In a NutShell. Bantam Books, Nov 2001.

Holika: www.indiaexpress.com/rangolia/holi/html

Janganatha, panditraja. The Flow of the Ganges Ganga Lahari. Indica Books, Varanasi, 2007.

Jansem, Eva. The Book of Hindu Imagery. Weisner Books, 1993.

Jansem, Eva. The Book of Hindu Imagery. Weisner Books, 1993.

Jones, Christopher. Big Ice. Publish America, 2003.

Lama, Dalai Lama. The Dalai Lama's Book of Love and Compassion. Thorsons, 2002.

Lewis and Jordon. Creek Indian Medicine Ways. University of New Mexico. Albuquerque, 2002.

Loy Krathong Festival: www.geocites.com/siamsmile 365/loigratongl/html

Marchant, Kerena, Sloan Frank, Gryspeeroff Rebecca. The Book of Hindu Festivals. Raintree, 2001.

Mckay, Alex. The History of Tibet. Routledge, 2005.

Monibot, George. Heat,. Allen Lane Penguin Press, 2006.

Moore, Patrick . Travellers in Space and Time. Doubleday and Company, Inc., 1984

Neihart, G John. Black Elk Speaks. University of Nebraska Press, 1988.

Olson, Carl. The Book of the Goddess Past and Present. Crossroad, 1986.

Pierre, Mark and Long Soldier, Tilda. Walking in The Sacred Manner. Touchstone, 1995.

Poole, Robert. EarthRise: How man First Saw The Earth. Yale University Press, 2008.

Postal, Sandra. Pillars of Sand. WW.Norton Company, 1999.

Some Patrice, Malidoma. Off Water and The Spirit, Penguin. 1995.

Standing Bear, Luther. The Land of the Spotted Eagle. Houghton Mifflin, 1933.

Sumiyoshi, S, ed.Nigerian Culture and Customs: A Walk Through Time. Koemar, 1996.

Suzuki, David and MC Connell, Amanda. The Sacred Balance. Greystone Books, 2002.

The Kwatuitl Winter Ceremony: www.geocites.com/wilow1 d/winter.html

Tibetan Festivals: www.accesstibettour.com/tibetan-festivals/html

Tzu, Lao. Tao Te Ching. Penguin, 1963.

Vanbeek, Walte. Dogon: Africa's people of the Cliff. Harry N. Abrams, 2001.

Wade, Davis. Light at The Edge of The World. Vancouver: Douglas & McIntyre, 2002.

Weiner, Jonathan. Planet Earth. Bantam Books, 1986.

West, Anthony. Serpent in The Sky: The High Wisdom of Ancient Egypt. Julien Press, Inc., 1987.

Journey's End

Remember that it is the small compassionate actions we take that really make a difference.

To find out more about Author, Omileye Achikeobi – Lewis and Derrick Lewis (the other co-founder of the Humanity4Water Campaign and Awards)

Visit

www.yeyeosun.com

Finally

I embrace the Dreamtime Awakening

www.ingramcontent.com/pod-product-compliance
Lightning Source LLC
Chambersburg PA
CBHW062357090426
42740CB00010B/1312